THE COMPANION TO THE PBS™ TELEVISION PROGRAM

Window to the Sea

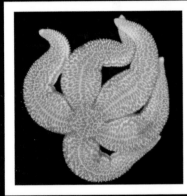   

Behind the Scenes at America's Great Public Aquariums

JOHN GRANT AND RAY JONES

INSIDERS' GUIDE®

GUILFORD, CONNECTICUT
AN IMPRINT OF THE GLOBE PEQUOT PRESS

INSIDERS' GUIDE ®

Funding for the *Window to the Sea* television program was made
possible by PBS and by John Arnold, Contemporary Ocean Artist.

Cover credits: front cover © Shedd Aquarium/www.fishphotos.org; back
cover (top, left to right) Monterey Bay Aquarium; Monterey Bay
Aquarium/Randy Wilder; © Shedd Aquarium/www.fishphotos.org;
Monterey Bay Aquarium; (bottom) Monterey Bay Aquarium/Randy Wilder

Text design by Linda R. Loiewski

Library of Congress Cataloging-in-Publication Data
Grant, John, 1948–
    Window to the sea : behind the scenes at America's great public
    aquariums / John Grant and Ray Jones.— 1st ed.
        p. cm.
    ISBN 0-7627-3970-3
    1. Aquariums, Public—United States. I. Jones, Ray, 1948– II. Title.
    QL79.U6G73 2005
    597.073'0973—dc22
                                    2005017611

Manufactured in the United States of America
First Edition/First Printing

TO LAURA STROM,
OUR FRIEND AND COLLEAGUE

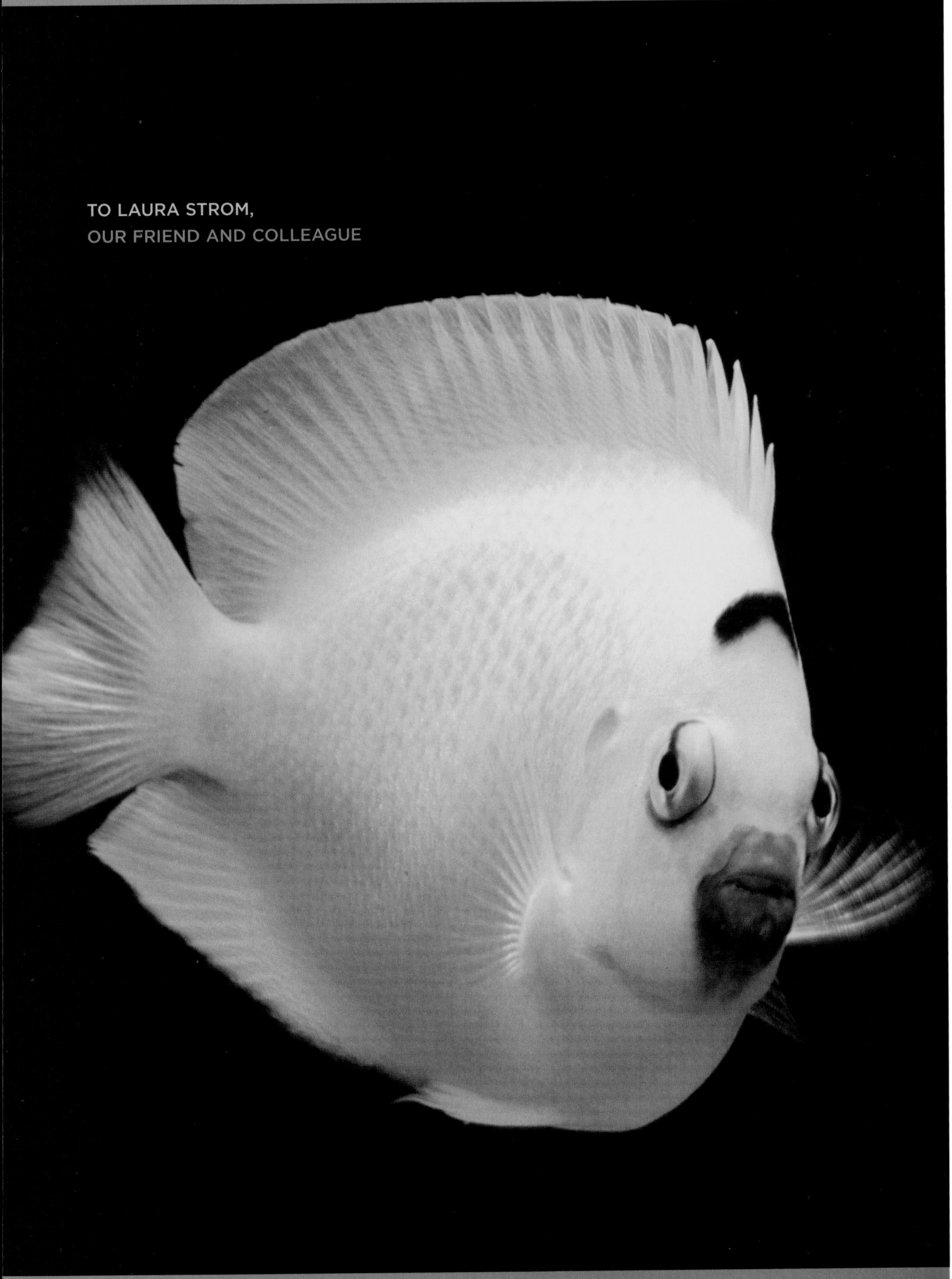

Contents

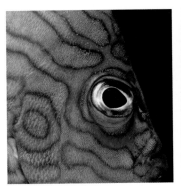

FISH MAKE UP AN INCREASINGLY SMALL PORTION OF AQUARIUM DISPLAYS. A PANTHER CHAMELEON IS NOT MUCH OF A SWIMMER, BUT LIKE MANY OTHER AIR BREATHERS—INCLUDING HUMANS—IT IS HIGHLY DEPENDENT ON THE AQUATIC WORLD.

Introduction

In Chicago, an all-white beluga whale frolics with dolphins in a giant pool beside a near-perfect re-creation of a northwestern seaside forest. In Boston a diver extends a hunk of cabbage as a 600-pound green sea turtle named Myrtle easily pushes aside a rainbow of tropical fish to insist on another bite of breakfast. In California, leopard sharks lurk in an onshore forest of giant kelp nourished by raw seawater pumped directly into their 335,000-gallon tank from nearby Monterey Bay. In Hawaii a man-made reef of many-colored coral grows so that natural reefs everywhere may survive.

Marvels such as these can be witnessed and enjoyed in public aquariums all across America. You can also sample them in this book and the exhilarating PBS documentary on which it is based. Both the television program and the book celebrate our nation's aquariums, their history, and the important educational and conservation roles they play.

As our title suggests, aquariums are meant to throw open a window to the sea—a portal into a magical and mysterious aquatic world that most of us can barely imagine. As you'll see, they serve this purpose extremely well. Where else is one likely to see jellyfish create living surrealist art? A dolphin stand on its tail? A pair of mating seahorses? A dragonfly that does its flying under the water? A school of silvery anchovies so numerous that even their keepers cannot count them?

Aquariums have always evoked wonder. From the first, that has been their primary function, but over time they have also become centers for vital scientific research. We know far more today about the world's oceans, lakes, and rivers than we did even a few years ago because of the painstaking work done in aquarium laboratories. Some of that knowledge may be used to save endangered species such as the right whale, monk seal, Kemp's Ridley sea turtle, or Florida manatee.

SURVIVAL IS THE OBJECT OF LIFE. THIS HAWAIIAN TURKEYFISH WARDS OFF MOST NATURAL THREATS WITH PORCUPINE-LIKE SPINES.

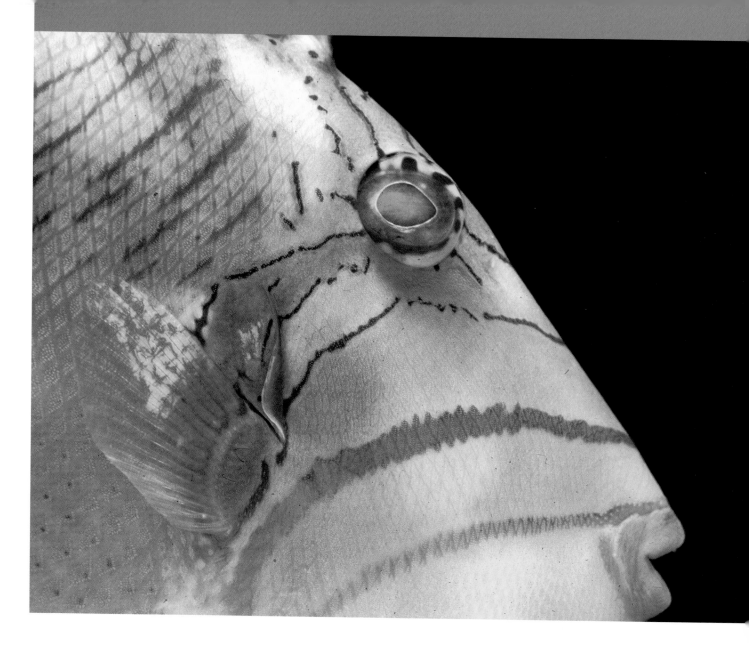

In fact, conservation itself has become a potent focus for aquariums. Nearly all sponsor or participate in conservation programs. Some help track sharks, rays, or seals. Others serve as hospitals for injured or stranded animals that need to take time out from the wild for rehabilitation. And every aquarium tries to convey a lucid and persuasive conservation message, usually similar to this: "Our oceans are fragile, and we must not abuse them."

Aquariums have changed considerably over the years and have broadened the scope of what they attempt to accomplish. In the beginning, however, they were little more than aquatic museums where people went to see strange-looking fish.

Aquariums of one sort or another have been around for thousands of years. The Chinese have been keeping goldfish since at least A.D. 265, and the rich or royal families of other nations have kept colorful fish in special pools or small garden tanks for centuries. However, public aquariums with fixed exhibits and glass-walled tanks did not appear until the middle of the nineteenth century.

The first widely known public aquarium opened in London's Regents Park in 1853, and during the next few years, several others were established in cities across Britain. All these early aquariums suffered from the same problem—their fish died at a depressingly rapid and costly rate. Most of these hapless creatures probably suffocated or perished from heat or cold, but before long aquarists had learned the necessary tricks of the trade such as aeration, filtration, and temperature control. Aquariums in the United States benefited from these hard-won lessons and were more successful, at least in keeping their animals alive.

Most of these early aquariums were modest operations with a few hundred fish and other animals gathered into tanks able to hold no more than thirty gallons of water. Compare that to today's Shedd Aquarium in Chicago with its 8,000 animals and three-million-gallon Oceanarium. Even so, by the late nineteenth century the public aquarium movement had become firmly established, and by the early twentieth century more than a few U.S. cities had aquatic display facilities. Major aquariums of the era in cities like Boston, New York, and Detroit were equal in size and popularity to those of today, but of course there were key differences.

Public aquariums in the United States have evolved significantly during the past century, and they fall into three distinct generations depending on when they were built or the style of their exhibits. First-generation aquariums, including nearly all those established

ONE MIGHT MISTAKENLY BELIEVE THAT A CREATURE LIKE THIS COWFISH COULD ONLY HAVE BEEN GENERATED BY COMPUTER.

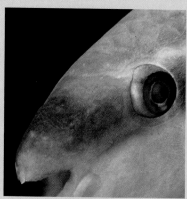

before the late 1960s, tended to display animals as though they were curiosities in a museum. Often they were shown against a black or solid-colored background to highlight their unique features; little or no attempt was made to depict the creatures' native habitats. This generation likely reached its zenith with the opening of the fabulous John G. Shedd Aquarium in 1929. Over the three-quarters of a century since, the Shedd has adopted many of the open, habitat-oriented display techniques developed by later generation aquariums, but a walk through its older galleries is like taking a trip in a time machine—a delightful one. You'll read much more about all that in Chapter 1.

The subject of Chapter 2 is Boston's New England Aquarium, often described as the first modern aquarium. When this innovative structure opened its doors in 1969, the second generation of the aquarium movement was off and swimming. Now exhibits were made to look as realistic as possible, and innovative designs gave visitors more access to the displays.

During recent decades a third generation of aquariums has begun to bring the ocean itself to the visitor. For instance, the Monterey Bay Aquarium, founded in 1984—and described in Chapter 3—supplies exhibit tanks with water pumped straight out of the bay. The bay water introduces nourishing invertebrates and algae—lifeblood of the ocean—to the tanks. In essence the exhibits become living extensions of the sea.

If there is to be a fourth generation of aquariums, perhaps they will be wholly scientific institutions devoted to ocean conservation. No aquarium is more committed to ocean stewardship than the one at Waikiki on Oahu in the Hawaiian Islands. Groundbreaking work has been done there in propagating coral, and this may lead to restoration of some of the richest marine environments on the planet. Ironically, founded way back in 1904, the Waikiki Aquarium is one of America's oldest public aquariums. You can get a revealing sense of this fine old aquarium's past—and maybe its future as well—in Chapter 4.

There are many reasons to visit an aquarium. Having fun is certainly one of them. Learning is another, and pitching in to protect ocean habitats is a third. But the most important reason to go to an aquarium is for ourselves. We spend so much of our lives peering at exteriors—the facades of buildings, the paint jobs on cars, the covers of books, the faces of people we pass on the street. At the beach, standing beside the primeval ocean we may rightly feel closer to the essence of things, but when we look out over the water, what we see there is a reflection. Aquariums offer us the chance get beneath the surface and, if we wish, to go even deeper. We'll see you there.

MILLIONS OF YEARS OF EVOLUTION HAVE GENERATED AQUATIC CREATURES IN EVERY IMAGINABLE SIZE, SHAPE, AND COLOR. THAT'S WHY AQUARIUM EXHIBITS ARE MUCH LIKE AN ARTIST'S CANVAS.

THE FORM OF A SEAHORSE IS
FAMILIAR TO EVERY SCHOOLCHILD,
BUT THE ANIMALS THEMSELVES
REMAIN SURPRISINGLY ALIEN.
AQUARIUMS BRING THEM OUT OF
THE WATERY SHADOWS.

CHAPTER 1

Weighing every bit of 2,000 pounds, an all-white beluga whale glides upward with a deliberate forward momentum.

John G. Shedd Aquarium

The beluga gently breaks the surface, and for a few seconds its enormous head and body generate a wake. Then the creature gracefully slips down the far side of the arc it is forming until it approaches the bottom and turns, once again, toward the surface. While the beluga continues its ballet, a nearby white-sided dolphin puts on a more vigorous performance, leaping completely out of the water, then dropping back nose first, producing a splash so subtle and controlled that it would earn respectable marks in a diving competition.

Scenes like these might be enjoyed along the coast of the Pacific Northwest—if the observers had sharp eyes and were very, very lucky—but in the Midwest? Indeed, the images just described can be seen and photographed within full view of Lake Michigan and only about a mile from Chicago's historic Loop District. This is the marine mammal pavilion at John G. Shedd Aquarium, one of the oldest and most respected facilities of its kind in North America.

A MIDWESTERN EXTENSION OF
THE WORLD'S GREAT OCEANS,
CHICAGO'S JOHN G. SHEDD
AQUARIUM IS HOME TO RARE
WHITE-SIDED DOLPHINS AND
MORE THAN 650 OTHER
MARINE SPECIES.

The Shedd was the world's biggest aquarium when it was built in 1930 and remains to this day a very impressive facility. Still the nation's largest indoor aquarium, it can boast tanks with an overall capacity of nearly five million gallons. While that's not an ocean, it *is* a lot of water, more than enough to support the Shedd's 650 marine species and thousands of individual fishes, reptiles, amphibians, mammals, and invertebrates.

One might very well ask how such a large and exceptional aquarium came to be located here more than 800 miles from the Atlantic and 2,000 miles from the Pacific. Part of the explanation lies in the fact that Chicago is, well, Chicago. The city was founded during the early 1800s, not by settlers moving slowly across the plains in wagons but by Great Lakes traders and shippers, who hoped to use it as a port to access the boundless resources of the West. Ever since then, Chicago has seen itself as linked to the rest of the country and the world by way of the Great Lakes and, today, in a very real sense via O'Hare Airport and the St. Lawrence Seaway. Local business writers are fond of referring to the Great Lakes region in general and to the Chicago area in particular as America's Third Coast.

Chicago has always been a city of superlatives. At one time or another it could claim the world's tallest building, the Sears Tower; largest commercial center, the Merchandise Mart; largest public library, with more than two million books; largest cookie factory, Nabisco; and largest department store, Marshall Field. The latter structure and the money it made for those who owned and ran it led indirectly to the founding of the Shedd Aquarium.

"The aquarium is named after John G. Shedd, one of the first CEOs of the Marshall Field Company," says Ted Beattie, who has served as Shedd Aquarium president and CEO for more than a decade. "Shedd was a close friend of Marshall Field, who was responsible for building Chicago's famous Field Museum."

Born in 1850, John Shedd began his business career as a $10-a-week stocking clerk for the downtown Chicago department store that would come to be called Marshall Field, for its founder. Working his way up in the company, Shedd eventually became a partner to Marshall Field, who died in 1906, leaving behind as a memorial the world-renowned Field Museum of Natural History. Shedd replaced Field as president of the company and years later gave thought to a memorial of his own—something he could leave to the city of Chicago. Shedd finally settled on the idea of a public aquarium, to be owned and operated by the city.

A Long Way from the Ocean

Given Chicago's considerable distance from the ocean and the fact that at the time there were very few public aquariums anywhere, this may have seemed an unlikely notion. Even so, encouraged by an initial Shedd donation of $2 million, city officials embraced the idea, and construction got under way in 1927.

Even during the heady 1920s, when things got done quickly, a facility as complex as the Shedd Aquarium could not be established overnight. It took more than two years to complete the mammoth Greek-style edifice, about the same time it would take New Yorkers to erect the Empire State Building (begun in 1929 and completed in 1931). Meanwhile more than a million gallons of seawater were brought up from Key West, Florida, in railway tankers. Then thousands of sea creatures had to be imported from all over the world.

A FIXTURE OF THE LAKE MICHIGAN WATERFRONT SINCE 1930, THE SHEDD (FOREGROUND LEFT) IS ONE OF AMERICA'S OLDEST MAJOR PUBLIC AQUARIUMS.

By the time the aquarium officially opened its doors to the public on Memorial Day in 1930, John Shedd had long since left the scene—he had died in 1926—and the Roaring Twenties had given way to the Great Depression. With the city having fallen on hard times along with the rest of the nation, the new aquarium gave Chicago a fresh and much-needed diversion.

"In those days, when Chicago built something it had to be the biggest—the tallest, the largest museum, and so on," says Beattie. "The aquarium was very substantial for its time."

PRESIDENT AND CEO TED BEATTIE SAYS HIS AQUARIUM IS PROUD OF ITS GLOBAL COLLECTION OF MARINE LIFE.

Located hard by Lake Michigan on a landfill created with debris left over from the Great Chicago Fire of 1871, the 200,000-square-foot aquarium was no less marvelous than it was sizable. Designed by well-known Chicago architect Daniel Graham, it reflected the thinking of Graham's mentor and former employer, Daniel Burnham, who had devised a master plan for the city during the early 1900s. Burnham had dreamed of turning Chicago into a "Paris of the Prairie." In keeping with that vision, which had influenced the design of the nearby Field Museum, Graham gave the city an aquarium building that in many respects resembled a Greek temple. At the entrance, Doric columns supported a portico approached by way of a broad stone staircase. In traditional Greek manner, the structure itself formed a cross, and it had a large central hall crowned by a dome.

However, Graham's design was by no means rigidly classical. It was lightened throughout by waves, fish, seashells, and other playful details typical of the Beaux-Arts movement then popular in Europe. Dolphins, turtles, and the gaping jaws of sharks enlivened the outer walls. In the rotunda, painted terra-cotta tiles depicted crabs and fish. Coral and lobsters covered the bronze doors at the entrance; just inside, bronze octopus tentacles wriggled down over the globes of hanging lamps, and a large clock told the time with stylized sea creatures rather than numbers. Visitors might arrange to meet under the clock at "a quarter to starfish" or "half past seahorse."

An early guide to the aquarium describes the effect as follows: *Wherever consistent with the classic design, various aquatic motifs were worked into the marble and tile. Fishes, turtles, shells, and invertebrates, all modeled from life, are seen on every hand.*

"The array of sea life portrayed on the outside of the building and throughout the interior is amazing," says Karen Furnweger. As editor and content manager for the Shedd, Furnweger gets plenty of opportunities to tell the aquarium's story and to describe its unique features. "You have sea turtles and shells, the snails, and aquatic plants portrayed along the cornice. There are cresting waves that go up the dome. And topping off our dome is Neptune's trident, which is sitting on top of four dolphins."

Like all fine architecture, the Shedd's extraordinary design and decor convey a message to everyone who walks through its doors. "When you enter the building," says Furnweger, "it's telling you that you are going to see the most amazing collection of aquatic life in the world."

Of course this astounding structure was intended not just as a celebration of aquatic life but to display it. Interestingly, little more than a third of the building was set aside for exhibits. The rest was filled with the innovative machinery and 75 miles of pipe that made it possible to monitor the exhibits and provide them with a constant supply of clean water heated or cooled to just the right temperature. All this supported displays filled with wondrous fishes and other marine animals that had never lived so far from the sea and that Chicagoans had never seen.

AT THE SHEDD THE FUN BEGINS EVEN BEFORE YOU SEE THE FISH. THE ENTRYWAY SUGGESTS A GREEK TEMPLE, PERHAPS DEDICATED TO POSEIDON, AND JUST INSIDE, A BIG BRONZE CLOCK SPORTS STARFISH, LOBSTERS, AND SEAHORSES INSTEAD OF NUMBERS.

The Shedd proved an immediate success, drawing 4.6 million visitors during its first full year of operation. It was and remains today the premiere attraction in a city that demands the biggest and the best. This was true not just because of the aquarium's size or design but also because at the Shedd, Chicago discovered a fresh and very profound link to the oceans and the world at large.

World's Aquarium

From the beginning, the Shedd's collections were planetary in scope. The idea was to display an array of sea creatures from distant seas and oceans. Visitors wanted to travel as far as possible from their humdrum and all too often hard-pressed day-to-day lives, and that's just what they could do at the Shedd. When Chicagoans stepped through its doors, few were disappointed.

"People wanted to see what was happening in the oceans of the world," says Bert Vescolani, Shedd senior vice president for aquarium collections and education. "So the Shedd gave them a menagerie of aquatic life from all over."

The aquarium tanks were filled with exotic species, many of them transported to Chicago in a specially designed railcar dubbed the *Nautilus* after the submarine in Jules Verne's novel *20,000 Leagues under the Sea*. Some sea creatures were brought from foreign ports aboard ocean liners and then transferred to the *Nautilus*. Others were collected by fishermen who worked the waters off the nation's Atlantic, Pacific, Gulf, and Caribbean coasts. Freshwater species, gathered from lakes and streams added to the mix and enabled the Shedd to become the first aquarium to maintain permanent exhibits of both saltwater and freshwater fishes.

"The original idea was to show a collection from around the world, and we've kept true to that," says Vescolani, who started with the aquarium as a high school volunteer and fell in love with the place. Having worked here professionally for more than thirteen years, he has never lost his fascination for the Shedd and the extraordinary variety it offers, both as an employer and as a showplace for marine life.

"On any given day I can be working with the animal collections staff, helping move sharks around, or walking through the aquarium with a group of school kids," says Vescolani. "What they and others see here are marine mammals, fish, birds, and amphibians from all over—a truly global collection."

In operation for more than seventy-five years, the Shedd is a venerable oldster as aquariums go. It was and, to a certain extent, remains today what some refer to as a "first-generation aquarium." It has always maintained a large number and diversity of exhibits, but originally they were small, designed to show off the colors and distinctive traits of one or two exotic species.

EDITOR AND CONTENT MANAGER KAREN FURNWEGER NEVER TIRES OF POINTING OUT THE FANCIFUL SHELLS, SHARKS, TURTLES, FISH, AND OTHER PLAYFUL BEAUX-ARTS DETAILS THAT MAKE THE SHEDD AN ARCHITECTURAL CELEBRATION OF SEA LIFE.

"When we opened our doors in the 1920s and 1930s, most aquariums had postage-stamp collections," says Vescolani. "Their displays were something like snapshots in a slide show. The style was to show a fish with some gravel and a backdrop. It was a black box, if you will, and it did show off the animal really well."

Since the days when the Shedd was built, display styles have changed significantly. Today there is more emphasis on habitat and how animals actually live in the wild. So-called second- and third-generation aquariums, such as the New England Aquarium in Boston and the Monterey Bay Aquarium in California, strive to convey a sense of a creature's true ocean environment. Nowadays, so does the Shedd.

With reverence for its past and a healthy sensitivity to the expectations of its visitors, the Shedd maintains exhibits in both the new, environmental style and the earlier "black-box" styles. The older Shedd galleries remain true to their origins, and a leisurely stroll through them allows visitors to step back into the past and see what aquariums looked like several generations ago during the era of jazz and Prohibition. Elsewhere in the aquarium, visitors are allowed to immerse themselves in a marine habitat. For example, the Shedd's popular Wild Reef exhibit strives to covey the experience of diving onto a real Philippine reef.

"I believe the Shedd Aquarium blends the old with the new really well," says Vescolani. "Our Amazon Rising exhibit provides a good example. The architec-

OLDER EXHIBITS PROVIDE A QUAINT HISTORY LESSON IN THE WAY EARLY AQUARIUMS AND THEIR VISITORS VIEWED SEA CREATURES.

ture is the original. We kept the vaulted ceilings and the old gallery design but blended it with new, state-of-the-art technology, animal care, and filtration. Combine all that with spilling of light and natural beauty, and you've created a forest that visitors can walk through."

Perhaps not entirely by coincidence, Amazon Rising harkens back to the Shedd's very first exhibit. A swampland scene arrayed in the unfinished rotunda, it delighted the public for months before the aquarium's

A PURPLE POISON DART FROG FROM THE RAIN FORESTS OF CENTRAL AMERICA.

official Labor Day opening in 1930. Now the Shedd delights and amazes its visitors with habitats reflecting those found in the world's greatest swamp—more properly described as a rain forest—the Amazon. In this way and others, the Shedd continues to update its approach but without abandoning its global vision.

"Many of the aquariums being built today are regional or have smaller collections focused on a single area or environment," says Vescolani. "We've keep animals from all over, and that's one of the reasons we're still the World's Aquarium."

Indoor Ocean

The Shedd remains an irresistible magnet for tourists in a city loaded with appealing places to go and things to do. More than two million visitors press through its doors every year. Many who come today, however, are less interested in exotic fish than they are in marine mammals.

NO MATTER HOW ALIEN THEIR APPEARANCE, AQUATIC CREATURES SHARE WITH US THE GIFT OF LIFE AND PERHAPS MUCH MORE.

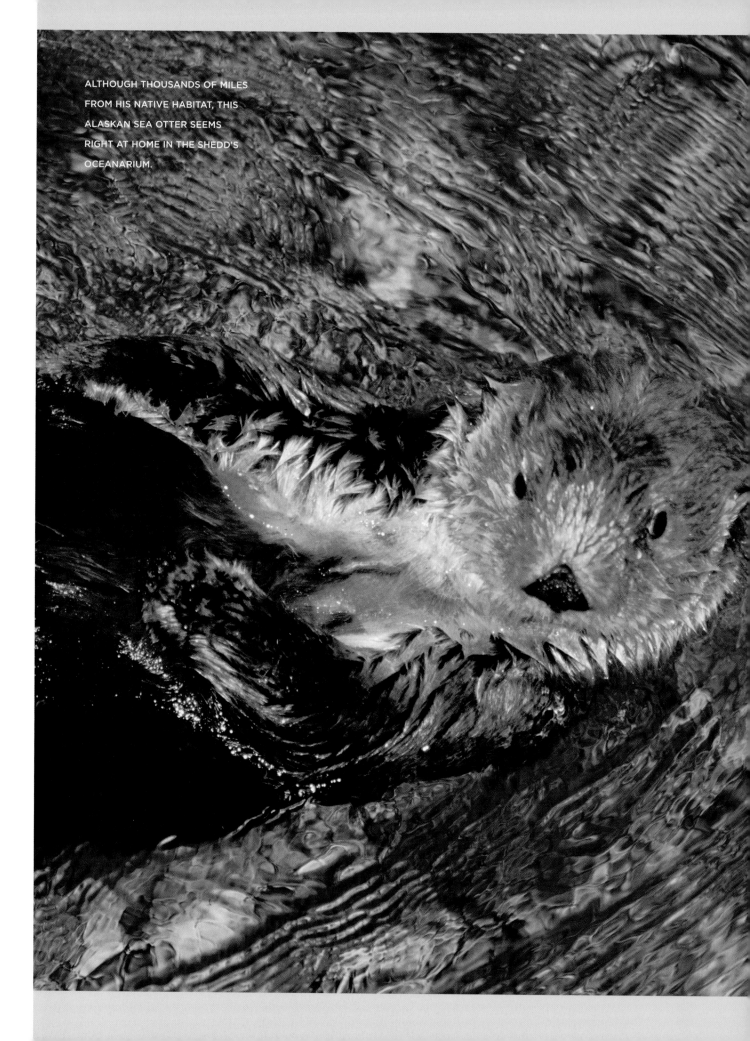

ALTHOUGH THOUSANDS OF MILES FROM HIS NATIVE HABITAT, THIS ALASKAN SEA OTTER SEEMS RIGHT AT HOME IN THE SHEDD'S OCEANARIUM.

By far the most popular part of the Shedd is its Oceanarium, where crowds of children and adults gather daily to be entertained by the antics of dolphins and sea otters and enthralled by the magnificence of whales.

The Oceanarium, with its three-million-gallon tank, was not part of the original aquarium. "It was one of our first big expansions," says Ken Ramirez, who joined the aquarium staff at about the time the Oceanarium was being built in the late 1980s and now serves as vice president for marine mammals and animal training. "For many years after we opened our doors in 1930, there was very little change. Then we realized that one of the things missing from our mission of educating the public about aquatic life was the story of marine mammals."

Erecting this mammoth structure was an undertaking nearly equal in scale to constructing the original aquarium. The project took two years and consumed enormous quantities of building material, including 11 miles of pipe, 129 miles of electrical wire and cable, 1,200 tons of structural steel, 3,350 truckloads of concrete, 20,000 square yards of glass, and 364 tons of salt. The latter commodity was required to create the three million gallons of salt water needed for the huge Oceanarium tank. The aquarium no longer brings its water from the ocean in tanker cars as it did in the beginning. Today aquarium staffers mix it themselves using fresh water from Lake Michigan and measured quantities of sea salts.

No ordinary expansion project, the Oceanarium effectively doubled the size of the old 1930s aquarium. And while it took about the same length of time to build, the Oceanarium cost more than ten times as much as the original structure—some $34 million. The new exhibit required all this effort and money because it aimed not just to display marine mammals but also to show how they lived in the wild. This represented a significant departure for the Shedd. A first-generation aquarium with old-style exhibits that emphasized individual species, it was now embracing the habitat-oriented display style of aquariums established in recent decades. Unlike the Shedd, many of these other aquariums concentrate on a given region, a relatively small slice of the planetary ocean environment.

"We wanted to create a habitat, a natural setting for our dolphins, whales, and otters," says Ramirez. "It made sense to choose a cold-water environment, so we selected the Pacific Northwest."

The Oceanarium experience begins with a walk along a gentle trail through a faithful re-creation of a northwestern coastal spruce forest. This leads to a broad gallery offering a topside view of the expansive Oceanarium tank and the exuberant creatures that live, splash, and play in its waters. A lower gallery allows visitors to see the tank just as its inhabitants generally see it, from below the surface. Both galleries provide face-to-face encounters with the new stars of the Shedd—the dolphins and whales.

BUILT DURING THE LATE 1980S, THE OCEANARIUM HAS BECOME THE SHEDD'S MOST POPULAR ATTRACTION. THE EXUBERANT ANTICS OF DOLPHINS, SEA OTTERS, AND OTHER OCEANARIUM SEA MAMMALS HAVE MADE THEM AQUARIUM SUPERSTARS. THEY OCCASIONALLY SHARE THE LIMELIGHT WITH WADDLING PENGUINS.

Whales Far from the Sea

Like the nemesis of Captain Ahab in Herman Melville's classic novel *Moby Dick*, beluga whales are white. However, belugas are different from Melville's monster—a giant sperm whale—in nearly every other way. They are not very scary and seem unlikely to sink a ship, even an early-nineteenth-century whaling bark such as the one Ahab sailed headlong to destruction in the Melville novel. These are more gentle creatures, although they can be endlessly fascinating and devilishly curious.

"They're wonderful animals," says Ramirez. "They've got a lot of character and personality. When people walk into the Oceanarium and see the belugas, it's often hard to tell who is watching whom. The whales see kids running around, people of different sizes and shapes dressed in different ways, and I think they find that entertaining."

Belugas take an obvious interest in their environment, even in aquarium visitors, and they often seem to be looking around as though something intriguing has

BELUGAS SEEM TO ENJOY THEMSELVES ALL THE TIME. THIS ONE APPEARS TO BE LAUGHING.

just caught their attention. Unlike most other whales, belugas have flexible necks, which they can bend to give them a better view of something. This also makes them more expressive than other whales. It's easy to imagine that they live happy lives since, like dolphins, they often seem to be smiling.

Although they "smile" a lot, belugas are quite different from dolphins when it comes to mobility. "Unlike dolphins, belugas don't have those tall dorsal fins on their back, so they move much slower in the water," says Ramirez. "Because they live in a cold-water environment, they have a thick layer of blubber. They're very heavy, which slows them down. They're just not fast-moving animals."

Their deliberate movements make the belugas graceful, but in the wild their lack of speed makes them an easy target for predators such as sharks and orcas. Consequently they are quite rare, especially so in aquarium exhibits. The Shedd is one of only eight aquariums in North America with belugas on display.

Some of the Shedd's six whales were taken from the wild, in this case the western Hudson Bay; others were born at the aquarium. To reduce pressure on wild populations, the Shedd maintains an active breeding program for a number of species, including the beluga whale and white-sided dolphin. Even rarer than belugas, white-sided dolphins are kept in only a handful of zoos and aquariums. The captive population in the United States numbers only twenty, and five of these can be found at the Shedd.

KEN RAMIREZ GOES HEAD-TO-HEAD WITH A BELUGA. WHALES ARE BRAINY CREATURES, NO LESS INTRIGUED BY US THAN WE ARE BY THEM.

"We have an exciting breeding program for our white-sided dolphins," says Dr. Jeffrey Boehm, the Shedd's senior vice president for conservation and veterinary services. Boehm oversees the aquarium's medical staff and breeding efforts.

"We can move animals from institution to institution to facilitate breeding. We can also use more sophisticated techniques like artificial insemination. That's a tried-and-true practice in domestic animal medicine, but here we're applying it to a wild species. There's still a lot to learn, and the more we can learn, the more we can be self-sustaining and help maintain these populations both in aquariums and in the wild."

Just a Small-Town Doctor

During his thirteen years at the Shedd, Boehm has spent much of his time learning. Most of the species he and his staff treat here have never before been seen in a veterinary clinic.

JEFF BOEHM ADVOCATES AQUARIUM BREEDING PROGRAMS TO REDUCE PRESSURE ON THREATENED SPECIES SUCH AS THE BELUGA.

LIKE MOST OTHER AQUARIUM ANIMALS, THE FROGFISH (LEFT), ANEMONE PORCELAIN CRAB (CENTER), AND FLAME TANG (RIGHT) ARE MARINE CREATURES UNABLE TO SURVIVE IN FRESH WATER. TO MIMIC THEIR NATIVE ENVIRONMENT, AQUARIUM STAFFERS ADD A COCKTAIL OF SALTS TO ORDINARY TAP WATER.

WATER, WATER EVERYWHERE

Whether it is 90,000 gallons for the Caribbean Reef exhibit, 750,000 gallons for the Wild Reef, or 3 million gallons for the Oceanarium, water is never far from the minds of the Shedd Aquarium staff. For one thing, they have to keep track of quite a lot of it. The original 1930s Shedd had a tank capacity of 1.5 million gallons, which seventy years ago may have seemed a veritable ocean. Today the aquarium's exhibits hold almost four times that much water, and all of it must be monitored, cleaned, and kept at just the right temperature.

Water quality is a critical element of any aquarium's health care system. Since the well-being of the animals is directly linked to the condition of the water around them, Shedd aquarists cannot take this issue lightly.

"We run 8,000 to 10,000 tests per month," says Al La Pointe, the Shedd's senior chemist and water quality manager. LaPointe oversees staff and volunteers who constantly analyze and monitor aquarium water to ensure the health of the animal population. "We make sure the quality parameters are within acceptable ranges in all our exhibits."

La Point and his staff have a big job, but fortunately they are assisted by state-of-the-art monitoring equipment and an extensive treatment system capable of cleaning the Oceanarium's three million gallons every two hours. Clean water is not their only concern, however. Salinity, chemical content, and temperature must match that of the waters the animals would encounter in their native habitats. "Our goal is to replicate the animal's natural environment," says La Point.

Creating a match for the waters on a coral reef off the Philippine Islands or in the deep ocean can be tricky, especially for an indoor aquarium in the Midwest. Unlike some coastal aquariums, most notably the Monterey Bay Aquarium in California, the Shedd cannot pump raw seawater into its exhibits. In fact, there is no seawater to be had in Chicago unless it is brought in on railway tanker cars, as was done in 1930 for the Shedd's early exhibits.

The Shedd no longer imports seawater, now mixing its own by combining fresh water from Lake Michigan with salt and other chemicals. Usually the aquarium uses a synthetic seawater mix known as Instant Ocean, which contains a number of chemicals, including magnesium chloride, sodium chloride, calcium chloride, and potassium chloride. This mixture can turn ordinary tap water into a heady cocktail almost identical to the seawater that, for instance, washes over a tropical reef in the Pacific. It took 122,000 pounds of Instant Ocean and about fifty hours of hard work to turn the 750,000 gallons of lake water that had been pumped into the Wild Reef exhibit into a shark-friendly and distinctly salty inland sea.

"Virtually 90 percent of our collection is novel—if not new to science, then certainly to veterinary medicine," says Boehm.

The learning process begins anew each day. Every morning, at about the same time many of the animals are enjoying breakfast, Boehm meets with his staff to see what the day has in store. "Ours is a robust practice," he says. "It's not unlike providing medical care to a small town. Every day there are deaths. Every day there are births. It's a dynamic collection of patients, and we have to know all of them well."

Boehm and his staff handle an endless variety of tasks and medical concerns, ranging from routine checkups to the treatment of sick or injured animals. On any given day, for instance, a dolphin may be due for an annual physical or a sluggish frog may be in need of a pick-me-up. Occasionally, more serious health issues arise.

Perhaps the Shedd's most famous patient ever is Bubba, a 140-pound Queensland grouper. Bubba's story was exceptional from the first, since he was acquired in a most unusual manner. In 1987 he was dropped off at

THE SHEDD'S JUMBO-SIZE QUEENSLAND GROUPER, KNOWN AS BUBBA, HAS BEEN SUCCESSFULLY TREATED FOR CANCER.

the aquarium reception desk in a small cooler, most likely by a small home aquarium owner who had taken on far more fish than he could handle. Bubba's popularity at the Shedd grew quickly, right along with his weight.

"He's the sort of animal that makes you want to go up and give him a big hug," says Boehm. "People love him."

The big grouper had found his niche, but then he came down with cancer. Aquarists noticed pimplelike pink growths on his forehead, and tests revealed a malignant tumor. Rather than allow Bubba to suffer or perish, the Shedd veterinarians removed the cancerous tissue and administered chemotherapy.

Boehm believes this may have been the first time a fish was successfully treated with chemotherapy. "Treating cancer in a fish was a novel opportunity," he says. "We use standard medical techniques here every day. What is unusual about our veterinary practice is that we are applying it to new and very different species."

Despite the chemotherapy, Bubba's cancer came back, forcing the vets to perform a second surgery. This time they removed a larger area of tissue, and the treatment worked. Bubba now spends his days in the shark tank of the Wild Reef exhibit. He's so big that the sharks just ignore him—even if aquarium visitors do not. A close look at Bubba today reveals a large indentation on his broad forehead, the result of his treatment.

Only about half the aquarium's patients are treated, as Bubba was, in the well-equipped Shedd animal hospital. The other half is treated right in the tanks where they live. In some cases this requires a considerable degree of cooperation from the patients.

Training for Good Health

If aquarium animals are to be medically treated and cared for on a regular basis, they must learn to cooperate with their human keepers. This is especially true of large animals such as whales, dolphins, or sharks, which even under ordinary circumstances could be dangerous. That is why much of the interaction between these creatures and members of the Shedd staff is in one way or another related to training.

When crowds gather in the Oceanarium to watch the Shedd's white-sided dolphins put on their dramatic performances, part of what they witness is intended as entertainment. But there's far more going on here than a carefully choreographed leaping and tail-walking demonstration. While the talented stars of the show take center stage near the middle of the pool, their less experienced cousins are working one-on-one with trainers in other parts of the huge tank. They must learn their lessons well—their good health, even their survival, may depend on it.

"We train because that is an important aspect of good animal care," says Ken Ramirez, who runs the Shedd's animal training program. "There really are four cornerstones to a complete animal care program. The first is good veterinary care. The second is good nutrition. You want to make sure your animals are fed well and that they're getting a balanced diet with the right supplements. The third is the proper environment, water temperature, air temperature, shade, or foliage. And the fourth component is a behavior-management program to teach the animals to assist in their own care."

Many aquarium visitors may believe the dolphins at the Oceanarium are trained like circus animals so that the show can go on, but nothing could be further from the truth. Instead, their training and performances are an essential part of their daily care.

"There are a lot of misconceptions about our animal training," says Ramirez. "I would imagine that if you asked people why we train the dolphins at the Shedd Aquarium, nine out of ten would say we do it to put on a show. But that's not why we train."

ALTHOUGH TRAINING MAY ENABLE DOLPHINS AND SOME OTHER AQUARIUM ANIMALS TO PUT ON A GOOD SHOW, ITS REAL PURPOSE IS TO ENCOURAGE COOPERATIVE BEHAVIORS THAT MAKE IT EASIER FOR STAFF TO PERFORM ROUTINE TESTS AND MEDICAL PROCEDURES.

SHEDD DOLPHINS ARE TRAINED
NOT JUST TO PERFORM SPEC-
TACULAR ACROBATICS BUT TO
ASSIST IN THEIR OWN HEALTH
CARE.

Aquarium training is extended to many animals that never appear in one of the Shedd's popular performances. "We train our penguins, and they're never part of a show," says Ramirez. "We train our harbor seals, and most people don't even know we have harbor seals. So why do we do it?"

Training provides a number of benefits. "For one thing, it allows us to give the animals exercise," says Ramirez. "For another, it provides mental stimulation, but the most important benefit is that it teaches cooperative behaviors."

A well-trained aquarium animal can be expected to cooperate when it requires special attention or medication. The Shedd training regimen has likely saved the life of Tique, one of the aquarium's white-sided dolphins. Tique readily responds to a call made by placing a target card at water's edge. After a few playful exchanges, the dolphin will bob obediently beside its trainer while an assistant pours a gallon of fresh water into its throat through a long tube. Tique has kidney stones, and the water helps treat this painful condition.

RIGHT WHALES PUT ON A THRILLING SUMMERTIME DISPLAY IN THE BAY OF FUNDY. HUNTED TO THE POINT OF EXTINCTION, THESE MAGNIFICENT MAMMALS ARE NOW EXTREMELY RARE. ONLY A FEW HUNDRED REMAIN IN THE NORTH ATLANTIC.

WHALE POPULATIONS

Since whales may be scattered across thousands of miles of ocean and spend much of their time under the water, counting them can be extremely difficult. As a result, estimates of worldwide whale populations vary widely. Still it is clear that these magnificent creatures are not nearly as numerous as they once were, and some species are endangered. Beluga whale numbers have dwindled in recent decades and now are estimated to range from 40,000 to 80,000 worldwide. And the once ubiquitous right whale may be approaching extinction: In the North Atlantic only a few hundred remain.

The list below provides population estimates for several other great whale species. The numbers were compiled by the International Whaling Commission, an agency established by treaty to regulate the hunting of whales for commercial or scientific purposes.

Blue whales	1,400
Bowhead whales	8,000
Gray whales	26,300
Fin whales	47,300
Humpback whales (northern)	11,570
Humpback whales (southern)	10,000
Pilot whales	780,000
Minke whales (Atlantic)	149,000
Minke whales (Pacific)	25,000

"We do a lot of our training right in front of the public, and we describe it to them," says Ramirez. "People can actually watch that process take place."

Often the training sessions are not particularly dramatic or spectacular, as when trainers are working with the beluga whales. Belugas require numerous repetitions of a desired behavior, often rewarded by food or other positive reinforcements. At least ten times a day, the staff plays with the whales in what is sometimes called the "blood-taking game." A trainer signals one of the belugas, and it approaches, offering up its tail. This facilitates the taking of a routine blood sample, a procedure that would clearly be impossible without the whale's active cooperation. Most of the time, no blood is taken, but the game reinforces cooperative behavior that will in time be very helpful to both the aquarium's medical staff and the whale.

Yes, They Do Eat Seafood

Good nutrition is vital to the proper care of the aquarium residents, who are as hungry as they are numerous. To feed the 8,000 aquarium animals, the Shedd staff must process and serve several tons of restaurant-quality seafood every day. Each animal must be fed a specific diet consisting of the appropriate type and quantity of food along with vitamins and supplements. Care is taken in feeding the animals to manage their growth and ensure that they are not overfed.

Here again, the Shedd's commitment to training animals is evident. Training involves building a strong, long-term relationship with an animal. Trust develops once an animal realizes it is going to be fed and cared for. Nowhere is that trust more apparent—and necessary—than at feeding time in the shark tank.

A ZEBRA SHARK CRUISES THE WILD REEF EXHIBIT. CONTRARY TO POPULAR BELIEF, SHARKS WON'T EAT JUST ANYTHING.

"The biggest challenge in dealing with the sharks is feeding them," says Mark Schick, who manages the Shedd's Wild Reef exhibit. "We want to make sure we give them the proper amount of food. You feed them too much, and they're going to get big, maybe too big for the exhibit. You don't feed them enough, and they're going to start looking at the other fish and thinking, *Hey, maybe I should be hunting*. So we're very specific about how much food we feed them."

In order to keep track of its diet, each of the aquarium's twenty-five sharks must be fed individually. The sharks have been trained to recognize and respond to a set of visual and auditory signals, usually an object with a special shape, which is tossed in the water, and a clicking sound, like two sticks being struck together. Having been signaled, the shark approaches, takes its food, and then goes on its way. Not surprisingly, there are not as many loving interactions between these animals and their trainers as are likely to be seen in the marine mammal tank at the Oceanarium. Still, the sharks are not all mouth, and they don't come thrashing up out of the water as though to take off a trainer's leg.

"People have this misconception that sharks are vicious predators," says Schick. "I think people are just impressed by those big, showy teeth. Actually sharks are very graceful animals. They eat when they're hungry, and that's it."

Contrary to the popular myth that they are mindless predators, the sharks at the Shedd Aquarium have been relatively easy to train. The zebra sharks in particular have responded well to training. Unlike the

AQUARIST HEATHER THOMAS USES A FLOATING TARGET AS A SORT OF DINNER BELL TO CALL A ZEBRA SHARK FOR FEEDING.

other, more aggressive species in the tank, they allow the aquarists to hold and examine them during the feeding process. This has proven a significant advantage in caring for the sharks; the trust the staff has developed with the animals assures they are cooperative during medical procedures.

"Our smallest zebra shark will come up and let us handle him," says Schick. "He'll lie on our arms, and we can roll him over. We can draw blood or do an ultrasound on him. He's learned to trust us and that we're not going to harm him."

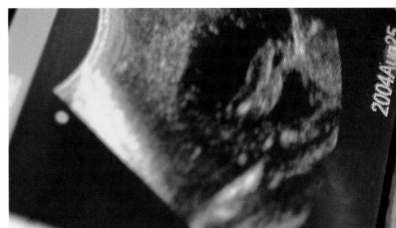

NAMED FOR THEIR DOLEFUL EXPRESSIONS, WOEBEGONE NURSE SHARKS ARE NOT VICIOUS PREDATORS, AND THEY BEAR LIVING YOUNG. THE WOEBEGONE ABOVE ALLOWED AQUARIUM VETERINARIANS TO REMOVE HER FROM THE WATER FOR AN ULTRASOUND EXAM (RIGHT), WHICH REVEALED THAT SHE IS PREGNANT.

A WALK-THROUGH IMMERSION EXHIBIT, THE WILD REEF PROVIDES A DIVER'S-EYE VIEW OF ITS CORALS, SHARKS, AND OTHER MARINE ANIMALS.

Diving onto a Reef

Sharks are the key attraction of one of the Shedd's newest and most exciting exhibits, the Wild Reef. Billed by the Shedd as an "encounter with sharks," the exhibit re-creates one of the world's richest ecosystems, a Philippine coral reef. An immersion experience, the exhibit's floor-to-ceiling windows allow visitors to plunge to the very heart of the reef—without getting wet, of course.

"The Wild Reef is a spectacular exhibit," says Bert Vescolani. "We were able to do something that we hadn't done in an aquarium-type exhibit. It's truly immersive. You walk in and you're surrounded by sharks and coral. They're over your head and down by your feet, and you see them in a new way. It's like being in the water with those animals. It's as close to a real diving experience as you can get."

With eight different interconnected habitats awash in 750,000 gallons of salt water, the Wild Reef is so large and diverse that it could never have been housed in the existing aquarium. Instead, a whole new wing had to be built. Only the second large addition to the Shedd since the aquarium was established more than seventy years ago, the new wing

THE 750,000-GALLON WILD REEF
EXHIBIT RE-CREATES A PHILIPPINE
CORAL REEF, PERHAPS THE
OCEANS' RICHEST HABITAT.

SCHOOLING ABOVE THE WILD
REEF CORAL, TROPICAL FISH
CREATE A LIVING WORK OF ART.

MANATEES IN OHIO

The Shedd's belugas and white-sided dolphins may be a long way from their native habitat, but they're probably no farther from home than the manatees at the Columbus Zoo and Aquarium in Ohio. This mid-western zoo/aquarium complex, likely more than 1,000 miles from the nearest wild manatee, has made these elephantine aquatic mammals a special focus. Not only are there three manatees in residence here—Dundee, Gene, and Turtle—but the aquarium partici-pates in a range of conservation programs aimed at saving this endangered species.

The Ohio manatees live in their own 190,000-gallon habitat known as Manatee Coast and are a hit with aquarium visitors, especially children. The youngest of the manatees is Turtle, an abandoned juvenile who was rescued near Satellite Beach, Florida, in 2003. The oldest is Gene, a 2,000-pounder born sometime before 1977, the year he was struck by the propeller of a small boat and brought to SeaWorld in Orlando for treatment. Because Gene was unable to survive on his own, he remained at SeaWorld, where he even-tually fathered Dundee, who was named for the movie character Crocodile Dundee. In 1999 Dundee and Gene were transferred to the Columbus Zoo and Aquarium as a replacement for rehabilitated mana-tees that had been returned to the wild. Now almost twenty years old, Dundee weighs in at 1,600 pounds.

Wild manatees eat—and eat and eat—an assortment of aquatic plants. In captivity they are fed heads of lettuce by the dozen and an impressive array and quantity of other vegetables. Despite their vegetarian diet, however, the manatees have no trouble putting on weight. Turtle weighed just 55 pounds when he was rescued, but during the next two years he gained nearly a pound a day and currently weighs about 700 pounds.

GENTLE GIANT MANATEES GLIDE JUST BENEATH THE SURFACE, A HABIT THAT MAKES THEM VULNERABLE TO POWERBOAT PROPELLERS. INJURED MANATEES HAVE BEEN REHABILITATED AT THE COLUMBUS ZOO AND AQUARIUM.

Fitted with a roof that retracts in warm weather to let in both sun and rain, the 22,000-square-foot Manatee Coast re-creates a mangrove habitat of the Ten Thousand Islands region in South Florida. Manatees were once plentiful in Florida's rivers and mangrove swamps, but no more. A distant relative of the ele-phant, the massive manatees are sluggish swimmers, and it is difficult if not impossible for them to get out of the way of speeding powerboats. Many are killed by the impact of the boat's hull or from cuts suffered when the propeller passes over them. The Columbus Zoo and Aquarium promotes conservation of this extraordinary but threatened species by providing a home for rehabilitating manatees and by helping track them in the wild.

was completed in 2003 at a cost of $47 million. The 27,500-square-foot structure was placed underground in order to preserve the architectural integrity of the original landmark aquarium building.

Wild Reef visitors will find themselves separated by just a few inches of crystal-clear acrylic from cruising predators—whitetip reef sharks, blacktip reef sharks, sandbar sharks, Japanese woebegone sharks, and zebra sharks, not to mention blue-spotted stingrays.

The exhibit also swarms with fish—emperor snapper, golden trevally jack, flashlight fish, coral catfish, and many other species. Additional exhibit highlights include a lush mangrove forest, a sea turtle nesting beach, and a re-created Filipino fishing village.

To put the considerable size of the Wild Reef exhibit into perspective, consider that the aquarium's much older but nonetheless marvelous Caribbean Reef exhibit, located in the main aquarium building, contains

THE WALK-AROUND
CARIBBEAN REEF EXHIBIT
UNDER THE SHEDD ROTUNDA
SYMBOLIZES THE AQUARIUM'S
WELL-ROUNDED APPROACH
TO LEARNING ABOUT AQUATIC
ENVIRONMENTS.

THE SHEDD HAS EARNED ITS REPUTATION AS CHICAGO'S MOST POPULAR DESTINATION BY BRINGING THE OCEANS OF THE WORLD TO THE MIDWEST AND BY CONVINCING VISITORS THAT THE RED-EYED TREE FROGS, TURTLES, AND HUNDREDS OF OTHER MARINE SPECIES AT THE AQUARIUM ARE NOT JUST CURIOSITIES—THEY ARE NEIGHBORS.

only about one-eighth as much water, some 90,000 gallons. Even so, the Caribbean Reef tank holds plenty of salt water to support bonnethead sharks, cownose rays, tarpon, and a rich array of other sea creatures. Each day divers enter the tank to interpret its wonders for crowds gathered on the other side of the windows.

"At one time Caribbean Reef was the largest saltwater aquarium tank in the world," says Vescolani. "It's hard to imagine now that an exhibit with 90,000 gallons was once seen as the aquarium of the future."

Interestingly, the aquarium's first exhibit—the rotunda "swamp" that introduced the public to the Shedd in late 1929—required comparatively little water. Even so, visitors were enchanted, just as they are today by the Shedd's endlessly varied and ever-changing efforts to bring Chicagoans, Midwesterners, and everyone else a little closer to their own watery planet. For the Shedd, the past and future are linked even as each of us—though we may not always be prepared to admit it—is tied to the sea and every creature in it.

CHAPTER 2

A lumbering leviathan breaks the surface of the sea and shoots a V-shaped spray of water into the air from a pair of blowholes.

New England Aquarium

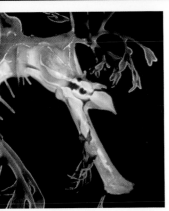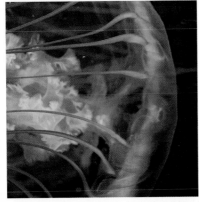

Then the giant dips its massive head and slips into the deep like a sinking ship going down by the bow. Before it vanishes, the creature bids farewell to the airy world above with a final, familiar wave of its huge tail.

This is a right whale, a big female, and spotting it is a thrill for Scott Kraus and his associates, who are watching from their research vessel on the Bay of Fundy, to the northeast of his late-summer base in Lubec, Maine, and near the most easterly landfall in the United States. Kraus has been tracking, tagging, photographing, and studying right whales for more than twenty years, but he still takes great pleasure in open-ocean sightings.

THE REACH OF AQUARIUM RESEARCH EFFORTS EXTENDS TO THE OCEAN DEPTHS, AND THAT IS JUST WHERE THIS RIGHT WHALE IS HEADED. WHEN A WHALE FLIPS ITS TAIL HIGH IN THE AIR, THE ANIMAL IS SOUNDING—THAT IS, GOING INTO A STEEP DIVE.

"Right whales are so rare that seeing one is almost a religious experience," says Kraus, who notes that, in this case, the word "rare" is an understatement. Only about 325 right whales remain in the North Atlantic, a population so low that it leaves the species teetering on the brink of extinction.

Several hundred miles from the bay, a poignant symbol of the right whale's plight can be found in Boston at the New England Aquarium, where Kraus serves as vice president of research. There are no living right whales at the aquarium, but a skeleton of one hangs from the ceiling near the entrance to the popular Giant Ocean Tank exhibit. Some 32 feet long, the articulated skeleton inspires awe in children and adults who can only imagine what such a large creature would look like in the flesh. Kraus knows, of course.

"It's shocking when you first see them," says Kraus, who runs the aquarium's North Atlantic Right Whale Research Project. "You are taken aback because they're so big and ugly. They're very unusual-looking creatures, with spiky callosities on their skin."

However, for Kraus and other right whale researchers, initial impressions have long since given way to familiarity. "The whales are so few in number that working with them is like living in a village," says Kraus. "You get to know every member of the community, and you feel every birth and death very acutely."

Lately, there have been more deaths than births, but this is nothing new. The right whale's fortunes have been spiraling downward for centuries. Once so numerous that legend has it you could walk across the water on their backs, they were wantonly slaughtered by whalers during the nineteenth and early twentieth centuries. Considered the "right whale" to hunt, these slow-moving marine mammals made easy targets for the harpoons of whalers, who converted their thick layers of blubber into high-priced oil. Even before 1935, when the League of Nations placed an international ban on the hunting of right whales, they had become so scarce that whalers had largely turned to other species. Since then, despite their protected status, right whale numbers have continued to dwindle. Unless the slide can be halted, these magnificent creatures will soon vanish from the oceans.

A PLUNGING ROCKHOPPER PENGUIN PROVES THAT WHALES ARE NOT THE ONLY EXPERT DIVERS AMONG THE MARINE AIR BREATHERS.

THE NOISY HOOTS OF HARBOR
SEALS DELIGHT BOTH CHILDREN
AND ADULTS AND KEEP THE
PUBLIC COMING BACK FOR MORE.

Fortunately, the big whales are not friendless. Preservation of the right whale, Kemp's Ridley sea turtle, and other endangered marine species is central to the mission of the New England Aquarium. As with other aquariums established in recent decades, it is part showplace for marine animals, part educational facility, and part research center. Its public education and research programs focus on the survival of endangered ocean species, especially whales.

"We're trying to help them," says Kraus. "Our focus is to keep them from going extinct."

AQUARIUM MEDICAL AND RESEARCH STAFFERS ARE WORKING TO SAVE THE ENDANGERED KEMP'S RIDLEY SEA TURTLE.

Boston's Extinct Aquariums

Ironically, aquariums themselves once seemed an endangered species in Boston. A number of early attempts to open and maintain public marine-life displays failed. Among these was one of the world's first publicly accessible aquariums, an establishment known as the Boston Aquarial Gardens.

Founded in 1859 by Henry Butler, an associate of famed showman P. T. Barnum, the Aquarial Gardens consisted of about forty modest tanks, not much larger than today's ordinary home aquariums. Arranged in a circle, these tanks held a variety of freshwater fish and sea creatures including starfish, crabs, carps, sea anemones, snails, periwinkles, sunfish,

sea ravens, flounders, rays, jellyfish, clams, pickerel, bass, and turtles. A larger central tank held a couple of sturgeons and a few perch. Handbills encouraged Bostonians to acquaint themselves with these "rare marine animals" and observe "LIFE BENEATH WATERS." Visitors were charged 25 cents for the privilege, a hefty admission price in those days.

Perhaps the price of a ticket was too high or underwater life was of less interest to Northeasterners than Butler had hoped. He soon beefed up the exhibits with cats, bats, monkeys, a muskrat, a raccoon, an opossum, a kangaroo, and other distinctly nonaquatic creatures. Even with the addition of a "man-eating shark" to its displays, the Aquarial Gardens did not long survive. Neither did the shark, which soon died, leaving the little aquarium without its prime attraction. During the early 1860s, Barnum bought out Butler and moved the aquarium animals to a new facility in New York.

Half a century would pass before Boston got another aquarium, this time a municipal facility located in South Boston's Marine Park. Completed in 1912 at a cost of $135,778, it had fifty-five relatively small tanks that presented fish in flat-panel style as though they swam in oil paintings hung on the walls. Exhibits were supplied by salt water pumped from a 100,000-gallon holding tank in the basement or by fresh water

DANGLING JELLYFISH TENTACLES WOULD NEVER HAVE BEEN SEEN IN EARLIER BOSTON AQUARIUMS.

straight from city taps. The aquarium stars were its large turtles, some weighing up to 200 pounds, and ever-popular seals, which were kept in a central pool. No effort was made to train the seals, but they barked and hooted with enough enthusiasm to keep the public interested. In fact, the South Boston Aquarium drew up to 15,000 visitors a day.

Unfortunately for the aquarium, it came into existence on the brink of very hard times for public institutions. During its entire forty-two-year run, spanning two world wars and the Great Depression, little was done to improve or update either the building or its exhibits. By the 1950s the aquarium was in deplorable condition, with nearly half its tanks empty, murky water choking the remaining exhibits, and one lonely seal left from its once vibrant and noisy colony. In 1954 the aquarium closed.

AT LEFT, A DIVER FEEDS ANIMALS BY HAND IN ONE OF THE BIG TANKS AT THE NATIONAL AQUARIUM IN BALTIMORE. BRILLIANT COLORS CAN BE FOUND NOT JUST IN THE AQUARIUM'S TROPICAL FISH DISPLAYS BUT ALSO IN ITS RAIN FOREST AVIARY (CENTER). THE AQUARIUM FEATURES AN ENORMOUS TANK THAT CAN BE VIEWED FROM SEVERAL LEVELS.

BALTIMORE AQUARIUM

The revolutionary architectural and display concepts pioneered by the New England Aquarium have been widely adopted by other facilities—perhaps nowhere more successfully than at the National Aquarium in Baltimore. Completed in 1981 as the centerpiece of Baltimore's Inner Harbor redevelopment project, the National Aquarium in Baltimore is a multistory structure with five levels of exhibits that offer visitors a linear, documentary-like experience. The similarity of this arrangement to that of the New England Aquarium is no coincidence, since both were designed by Peter Chermayeff and his firm, Cambridge Seven Associates.

In Baltimore Chermayeff significantly expanded on his New England design. At 335,000 gallons, the Atlantic Coral Reef tank is more than half again as large as the one in Boston, and there are more and larger galleries to visit as one ascends or descends each level. The journey carries visitors from the lobby level with its separate 265,000-gallon pool filled with small sharks and rays into Maryland's Chesapeake watershed with its blue crabs, terrapins, and spadefish. Beyond that lies a seabird aviary complete with razorbills, black guillemots, and puffins; the Amazon River basin exhibit with turtles and dazzling tropical fish; an upland tropical rain forest exhibit with iguanas and piranhas, and an open-ocean tank patrolled by bigger and more menacing sharks than those seen below.

The theme running through all this is "Without water there would be no life," an idea brought into clear focus by a gallery devoted to adaptation and survival. Here one encounters sturgeon and gar, primitive fishes that have changed hardly at all since the age of the dinosaurs; lionfish, which have evolved spines loaded with protective venom; giant Pacific octopuses, which can hide themselves in a cloud of ink; and highly specialized electric eels, able to stun their prey and enemies with a high-voltage shock.

Like many other large public aquariums today, this one has added a sizable marine mammal exhibit. Accessed via a bridge leading from the lobby level, it features a 1.3-million-gallon pool where bottlenose dolphins educate visitors while cooperating with the trainers who care for them. The aquarium added a substantial new wing to house a groundbreaking exhibit called Animal Planet Australia: Wild Extremes. Featuring creatures rarely if ever before displayed on this continent and re-creations of aboriginal art, the new exhibit is intended to demonstrate the strong bonds that link water, land, and culture.

Back from the Brink

The right whale and the New England Aquarium are linked—not just by a research program but also, perhaps, in spirit. The whales must recover as a species, a process that may prove a long and shaky climb. The aquarium has proven, though, that recovery and renewal are possible.

In 1969, fifteen years after its predecessor had expired from terminal neglect and dilapidation, along with most of the businesses in Boston's harbor district, the new aquarium opened its doors to a curious but wary public. Construction of the aquarium on a deteriorated wharf had defied odds, maybe even good business sense. At the time it was being planned and funded, entirely by private donors, most in Boston had given up on the downtown area and moved out to the suburbs. Even so, a small core group of aquarium supporters looked at the undesirable, rundown waterfront and saw what it might become. One of these visionaries was David Stone, who believed the aquarium would act as an economic catalyst for redevelopment of the harbor.

Stone envisioned creating a nonprofit aquarium that would excite people and reacquaint Boston with one of its most important resources—its historic waterfront and link to the Atlantic Ocean. Today the New England Aquarium is part of a bustling business and residential community jammed with attractions and activities that draw thousands of visitors, but its

DAVID STONE WAS ONE OF SEVERAL BOSTON VISIONARIES WHO SOUGHT TO REVIVE THE HARBOR DISTRICT BY FOUNDING AN AQUARIUM.

transformation did not occur overnight. It began in 1956, when a small group of civic leaders and businesspeople gathered to mourn the passing of the city's former aquarium.

"We got together on the second anniversary of the death of the old Boston Public Aquarium in South Boston," says Stone, a financial management consultant. "We hoped that at some point we could build a new, larger, more modern aquarium with a broader slate of objectives than the original one."

A VIRTUAL PORCUPINE OF THE DEEP, THIS PUFFER LIKELY HAS VERY FEW ENEMIES—OR FRIENDS. AT RIGHT, AN ANGELFISH INSIDE THE AQUARIUM'S TRADEMARK GIANT OCEAN TANK.

BOOSTED BY TOURISM AND OTHER BUSINESS GENERATED BY THE AQUARIUM, THE ONCE-RUNDOWN BOSTON HARBOR ENJOYS A RENAISSANCE.

As it turned out, one of those objectives would be redevelopment of the city's blighted waterfront. The New England Aquarium was to become one of the first in the United States to serve as an economic engine for revitalizing an inner-city area.

"Boston's waterfront was in an appalling condition," says Stone. "Its rotting wharves were caving in, and there was no pedestrian traffic down there whatso-ever. We hoped an aquarium would change all that by drawing people and reconnecting the city with the sea."

Although more than decade would pass before they could make the new aquarium a reality, supporters of the concept never gave up on their dream. With the assistance of the Boston Redevelopment Authority, the chamber of commerce, the mayor, and an assort-ment of city civic and financial leaders, the aquarium project slowly took shape. Funding was a major concern, especially since this aquarium, unlike its predecessor, was to be paid for entirely by private donations.

"As a new institution, we had no endowment; we had to wear out some shoe leather to raise the money," says Stone. "We had to raise $6 million. That doesn't sound like much today, but in 1960 it was quite a lot. It looked to us like a mountain of money."

Eventually, however, the money was raised and the aquarium built. Its doors opened on June 30, 1969, almost fifteen years after the old public aquarium in South Boston had closed. As Stone and other aquarium supporters had hoped, its impact on the waterfront was immediate and profound. Soon other develop-ments followed the aquarium to the harbor. Among the first were a pair of residence towers, which along with the aquarium itself generated fresh pedestrian traffic and helped attract new shops and businesses to the area. So too did a new city park and federal office complex, and in time the vitality of the harbor district had returned.

Waterfront Revival

The restoration of the area even extends to the harbor waters. Once a very active seaport, the harbor fell into decline after World War II, but centuries of use and abuse had left the harbor basin in a sad and all too often polluted state. Once redevelopment of the shoreline began, however, visitors could see more on the water than freighters and tankers. There are still commercial vessels, but during warm-weather months a gaggle of sailboats, yachts, and other small boats share the harbor. Boston Harbor is attractive once again, and there is far less pollution.

could survive, and you could barely see them," says Stone. "On the clear-water side there were several varieties of fish, and that was the harbor we envisioned."

The exhibit was accompanied by a map marked by small red lights indicating sources of pollution, such as storm drains and sewers that emptied directly into the harbor. Over the years, as the city eliminated these pollution hot spots, the red lights were exchanged for blue ones.

"As a result, people began to understand the scope of the problem," says Stone. "In a broader sense, it was all part of our effort to inform citizens young and old about our blue planet."

New Generation Aquarium

The founders of the New England Aquarium took a broad view of its mission. Unlike earlier aquariums in Boston and elsewhere, it would not only display aquatic life but also promote conservation of the oceans that supported that life in the wild. Achieving the aquarium's education, research, and conservation goals, while taking in enough ticket revenues to keep the doors open, required construction of a very unusual facility.

"We believe that an aquarium is really a gateway to the ocean," says Greg Stone, the aquarium's vice president for global marine programs. "The animals in the aquarium are ambassadors for their wild relatives."

The aquarium is partly responsible for this. As it turned out, revival of Boston's urban waterfront environment was closely linked to the aquarium's mission to educate and inform the public about marine life and the underwater environment. Stone says one early aquarium exhibit had a particularly powerful impact on public perception of the water in the city's harbor. The exhibit was relatively simple, consisting of a divided tank—one-half of it filled with clean water and the other half with murky water taken directly from the harbor.

"On the harbor side, only a couple of varieties of fish

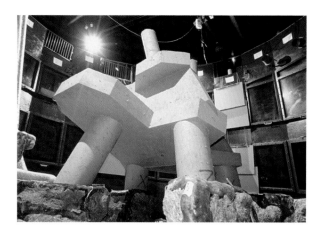

THE AQUARIUM'S SPIRAL WALKWAY AND OTHER INNOVATIVE DESIGN FEATURES MAKE POSSIBLE AN IMMERSIVE, DOCUMENTARY-LIKE EXPERIENCE.

To design a building that would help the animals play their roles as emissaries from the deep, aquarium planners turned to a young architect named Peter Chermayeff. At the time, Chermayeff was dabbling in film after graduating from Harvard and was not even sure he wanted to work as a structural architect.

"I was more interested in documentary filmmaking," says Chermayeff. "I hardly knew what an aquarium was other than what I had learned from my own tiny fish tank at home."

However, this project did interest him. He set about learning as much as he could about aquariums, how they were designed, and why. In the end, he took what he describes as a "multidiscipline" approach to his design for the New England Aquarium—a structure that was nothing short of revolutionary. In effect, the building he helped create was a living documentary of concrete, glass, water, light, and sea life.

"Other aquariums had presented their exhibits as though they were postage stamps in a collector's album," says Chermayeff. "We took a different path. We wanted a basketlike structure that the public could enjoy and experience on different levels in spiral fashion. So we created galleries providing views of four separate zones in the water. Those four zones became four floors, which we then wrapped around our central tank."

Chermayeff's design called for the building to be constructed around the aquarium's largest tank, some 40 feet in diameter and 21 feet deep. So big that it is often called the Giant Ocean Tank, it re-creates the rich environment of a tropical coral reef.

The tank's unusual depth presented technical problems because of the substantial pressures generated toward the bottom. "Dealing with the pressure was quite a trick," says Chermayeff.

Acrylic has become the standard material for assembling large aquarium tanks, but this extremely tough polymer was not yet available in the 1960s. Chermayeff and his builders were limited to laminated glass, which was cut into 4- by 6-foot panels to provide optimum viewing space for aquarium visitors. The tank itself also had to withstand the pressure, and the project's structural engineer came up with a solution. Using concrete he created a structure held together much like a whiskey barrel. The liquid inside the tank generates the outward forces that seal and tighten its concrete walls.

The spiral design made it possible for each visitor or small group to have their own window—a private niche where they could stand and peer into the depths. "We wanted them to feel as if they were underwater," says Chermayeff, "as if the water was all around them."

PETER CHERMAYEFF'S EXTRAORDINARY DESIGN BRINGS ARCHITECTURE, WATER, AND SEA LIFE TOGETHER IN SUCH A WAY THAT VISITORS FEEL THEY HAVE ENTERED A FANTASTIC BUT NONETHELESS NATURAL REALM BENEATH THE OCEAN SURFACE.

Indeed, the big tank lends that feeling to the entire building as light from the windows falls on adjacent walls. The shimmering aqua light creates the impression that the whole aquarium is alive—that the creatures inside the tank might very well swim out onto the ramps and join the crowd of human visitors. Side galleries continue the immersive experience for visitors, taking them to environments typical of far off oceans, seas, and lakes.

Chermayeff's design allows visitors not just a fleeting glimpse through a window at ocean life but also a chance to submerge themselves in the world those creatures inhabit. In part because of its extraordinary design, the New England Aquarium has been variously described as an "aquatic museum" or a "museum with living displays." It is also widely considered the first truly modern aquarium. Built nearly forty years after Chicago's Shedd, it represented a whole new generation of aquariums and served as a stepping-stone from earlier institutions to later ones, such as the Monterey Bay Aquarium, which in time would take aquarium evolution another step forward.

THE NATURAL APPEARANCE OF ROCKS IN THE GIANT OCEAN TANK MAKE THIS PROWLING SANDTIGER SHARK SEEM ALL THE MORE MENACING.

A CONVERSATION WITH PETER CHERMAYEFF

Peter Chermayeff's innovative design for the New England Aquarium earned him considerable acclaim. Since the aquarium opened in 1969, Chermayeff and the architectural firms he founded and works with have been commissioned to design at least a dozen zoos and aquariums. Among the more prominent of these projects have been the National Aquarium in Baltimore with its unifying themes; the Ring of Fire Aquarium in Osaka, Japan, with its red glass roof symbolizing a volcanic eruption; the Tennessee Aquarium in Chattanooga, which at first was devoted exclusively to freshwater species; and the Oceanario de Lisboa (Lisbon) in Portugal, which features a square display tank 100 feet across. Chermayeff's later work has taken full advantage of improvements in construction techniques and new materials such as acrylic. In step with these advances, Chermayeff's designs have evolved along with his thinking on exhibits and what they should convey to aquarium visitors.

ARCHITECT PETER CHERMAYEFF HAS DEVOTED MUCH OF HIS CAREER TO THE DESIGN OF AQUARIUMS AND ZOOS.

RECENT CHERMAYEFF DESIGNS BRING MARINE ANIMALS ALMOST CLOSE ENOUGH TO TOUCH.

"I've come to feel [the New England Aquarium] was a breakthrough," Chermayeff says, "not so much because of its physical shape and configuration or because it's a three-dimensional exhibit experience, but because it made a connection between education and fun."

About learning how to design an aquarium, Chermayeff says: "You learn enough to know what you don't know and who the experts are you can rely upon. The hardest part is learning to integrate architecture and interpretive exhibits with life-support systems for the animals.

"What we did in New England, we did more of in Baltimore," he says. "We brought exhibit design and architecture closer together and got a little more sophisticated because we could use acrylic (unavailable when the New England Aquarium was built during the late 1960s). We also started to think more about how people responded to interpretive information."

Aquarium exhibits are definitely getting bigger, Chermayeff says. "Our 40-foot New England tank was considered big in 1969, but by the time the Baltimore Aquarium opened in 1981, that was not big at all. Our aquarium in Lisbon, completed in 1998, has a square tank 100 feet across. We extended the corners into other habitats, which made the whole thing seem even bigger."

Chermayeff supports the movement toward more natural aquarium displays. "Combining species in more natural systems improves the experience for visitors—they learn more—and it's better for the animals," he says. But he's not so supportive of animal performances.

"Those shows are popular," he says, "but for many years my view has been that the dolphin show is not only obsolete, it's also demeaning to the animals. It's so much better to watch dolphins interact with one another without even being aware of us."

Diving on New England's Caribbean Reef

When it opened in 1970, a few months after the aquarium itself, the Giant Ocean Tank was the largest circular saltwater tank in the world. This 200,000-gallon masterpiece was the heart of Chermayeff's design, and it remains the centerpiece of the aquarium. It holds 130 different species and more than 700 animals in all. Its fifty-two large windows allow visitors multilevel views of sea turtles, eels, sharks, and other tropical fish typically found on a Caribbean coral reef.

Teeming with life and color, Caribbean reefs are wildly popular with divers. Holly Martel-Bourbon considers herself lucky to be able to enjoy an experience similar to that of a Caribbean diver nearly every

AQUARIST HOLLY MARTEL-BOURBON HAS BEFRIENDED HUNDREDS OF SEA CREATURES, EVEN MORAY EELS.

day—and without leaving Boston. It's part of her job as the senior aquarist and diving safety officer for the New England Aquarium, and she dives into the Giant Ocean Tank frequently.

"In some ways it's better than the Caribbean," says Martel-Bourbon. "You could never see this many animals on one ordinary dive in the wild."

Martel-Bourbon spends almost as much of her day underwater as above, but she enjoys working with the animals in the tank. To prepare for a dive, she sits on a small ledge at the top of the tank. A day's work may include feeding a large variety of species, monitoring their health and fitness, or cleaning and maintaining the tank, as well as helping increase public awareness and understanding of the marine environment. Visitors may be awestruck to see her swimming with sharks.

"People love sharks, so they usually come looking for the shark tank," says Martel-Bourbon.

Although the big tank is home to a couple of shark species and three species of rays, Martel-Bourbon insists that it is not really a shark tank. At one time the tank had more sharks and was dominated by predators, but their numbers have been downsized and the variety of animals increased to include tiny gobies, black cat basslets, Creole fish, and many of the other less menacing species that might be found on a Caribbean reef.

The water in the tank is continuously refreshed with harbor water that has been thoroughly cleaned, filtered, and heated to seventy-seven degrees—about the same temperature as Caribbean seawater. Conditions in the Giant Ocean Tank are, of course, much different from those divers might experience in the frigid waters off Boston—if they could stand the cold. Consequently, animals for the exhibit are collected in the Bahamas, not in the North Atlantic. So, in effect, the aquarium has brought to New England an exotic living sample, a slice of life in a far-off tropical sea.

"In a lifetime most people may not get to snorkel or scuba in the Caribbean, so we're bringing it here to show them the amazing diversity of the Atlantic," says Martel-Bourbon. "It's a very dynamic exhibit because there is so much to see. You can come back here every week and see something completely different each time."

Myrtle the Green Turtle

One creature visitors are invariably anxious to see is the Giant Ocean Tank's most famous resident and undisputed queen—a green sea turtle named Myrtle. Some say Myrtle is a holdover from the former municipal aquarium in South Boston, but no one seems to know for sure. While her background may be in doubt, her size certainly is not. She's big. Weighing in at better than 600 pounds, Myrtle's presence can be dominating.

MARTEL-BOURBON LIKENS HER EXPERIENCE INSIDE THE GIANT OCEAN TANK TO A DIVE ON A WILD CARIBBEAN REEF. USING AN UNDERWATER MICROPHONE SHE IS ABLE TO SHARE HER ADVENTURE WITH VISITORS OUTSIDE THE EXHIBIT.

MARTEL-BOURBON FEEDS MYRTLE, A GREEN SEA TURTLE
WEIGHING NEARLY ONE-THIRD OF A TON.

"She definitely owns the tank," Martel-Bourbon says of the big turtle. "She is by far the largest animal in the exhibit, and she is very much a personality."

Myrtle is very curious and extremely interested in food, and occasionally she gets in the way when it's time for other animals in the tank to eat. Given her considerable size, it's not always easy to discourage her.

"She can drive me nuts sometimes," admits Martel-Bourbon, who believes that after years of diving in the tank, she has developed a close relationship with Myrtle. The turtle responds to her mannerisms and hand gestures underwater as naturally as a person might respond to verbal commands. Training Myrtle is easy, since the turtle is obsessed with the food she receives as a reward.

Myrtle eats a lot of lettuce, but she also wolfs down other vegetables, such as red peppers, broccoli, cabbage, and brussels sprouts. A study of green sea turtle diets has shown that some vegetables contain nutrients similar to those in the vegetation a turtle would eat in the wild. For instance, red peppers are nutritionally similar to the turtle grass Myrtle might have grazed on in the ocean. Like other turtles in the tank, Myrtle also needs protein. In addition to her daily five pounds of salad fixings, she gets about half a pound of protein in the form of jellyfish, squid, and fish.

Hospital for Fish

Providing health care for such a large variety of species is demanding work and requires a state-of-the-art medical facility. The New England Aquarium medical center is one of the best and one of only a few such facilities that allow the public to view medical procedures. The center is, in fact, an aquarium exhibit—the first to show real staff and medical treatments to all visitors.

When the center opened in 1997, windows were installed so that visitors could observe routine examinations as well as more serious procedures. An overhead camera captures operations live and projects them onto screens to provide a closer view, while computer stations throughout the exhibit provide details on the patient's anatomy and condition.

"The aquarium medical center is unique because it brings veterinary medicine directly to the public," says Scott Weber, the aquarium's head veterinarian. "It gives us an opportunity to share with the public what goes on behind the scenes in the veterinary department."

There is plenty for people to see. Every year the center performs hundreds of routine exams and treats animals for ailments ranging from broken bones to pneumonia.

A PATIENT AFRICAN PENGUIN UNDERGOES A ROUTINE
MEDICAL EXAMINATION AT THE STATE-OF-THE-ART
AQUARIUM CLINIC.

Patients receive the highest quality care from a staff of nine veterinarians, veterinary technicians, biologists, and water quality specialists, as well as interns and volunteers who can expect to learn much by working in this very unusual animal hospital.

To diagnose animals, veterinarians take blood, skin, or scale samples to gather information. The quality of an animal's environment can be checked by testing for levels of algae and other organisms. Diagnosis also includes using imaging technology, such as X-rays, ultrasound, endoscopes, CAT scans, and video technology, which can provide an interior view of an animal's soft and bony parts.

If a sick animal requires an operation, visitors usually will be allowed to watch. When an audience gathers at the center to watch a surgical procedure, Weber narrates, carefully explaining each step. He estimates that as many as a hundred people will show up to see surgery performed on a fish.

The center's staff not only cares for the aquarium's collection but is also in charge of the rescue and rehabilitation program for stranded animals found on New England beaches. Often the center takes in injured and sick animals for short stays for rehabilitation before releasing them back into the wild. Rescued sea creatures that can no longer survive in the ocean may take up residence at the aquarium.

SCOTT WEBER TAKES SPECIAL PLEASURE IN HIS ROLE AS AQUARIUM VETERINARIAN, A JOB THAT OFFERS AN ENDLESS VARIETY OF CHALLENGES.

Rescuing Ridleys

Twice a year, Weber and his staff give the rare Kemp's Ridley sea turtles living in the aquarium a physical exam. Usually this is done at the side of the Giant Ocean Tank where the turtles now live.

"Kemp's Ridleys are among the rarest and most endangered sea turtles," says Weber. "We're very fortunate to have them at the aquarium."

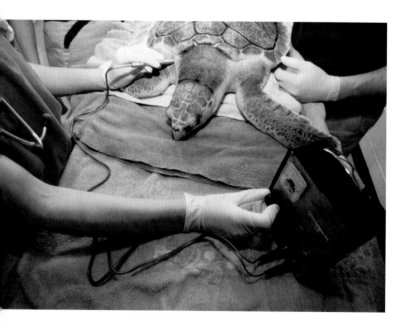

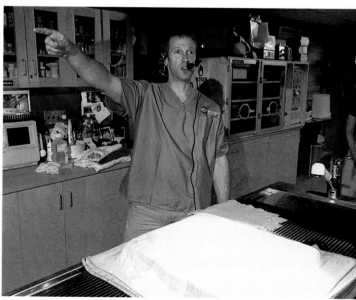

THE BIG SEA TURTLE AT LEFT HAS PROBABLY HAD MORE PLEASANT DAYS, BUT IT'S IN GOOD HANDS ON THE CLINIC EXAMINATION TABLE. AT RIGHT, WEBER TELLS VISITORS ABOUT HIS NEXT PROCEDURE AT THE CLINIC, WHICH DOUBLES AS AN AQUARIUM EXHIBIT.

The smallest of the Kemp's Ridley turtles at the aquarium was rescued several years ago. Her name is Scoot. Found on a beach in November 2000 by members of the Massachusetts Audubon Society, she was brought to the aquarium for treatment. Scoot's body temperature was forty degrees, so she was practically frozen. She had a heart rate of only four beats per minute, was severely dehydrated, and had also sustained injuries to both her front and back flippers. She was in such bad shape that the center staff began emergency treatment as soon as she arrived. She was given fluids, and her body temperature slowly increased over the course of a week. Later it was determined that Scoot also had bacterial and fungal pneumonia, which too was successfully treated.

"The Kemp's Ridley sea turtles really do have a special place in our hearts," says Weber. "During the course of a year we may rehabilitate any-where from fifty to a hundred of these rare animals."

Most of the rescued turtles treated at the center are brought in during the late fall. Like Scoot, these turtles become stranded on New England beaches, likely after having been swept off course by a storm and deposited in the frigid North Atlantic, where the water temperature is low enough to immobilize them. Once stranded, a turtle's only hope may be rescue and treatment at the aquarium. Every turtle saved in this way may be vital to the ultimate survival of this threatened species. Counts conducted during the 1990s indicated only about 5,000 nesting Kemp's Ridley females remained. Of these, a significant portion—as many as 1,000—have been treated at one time or another at the aquarium medical center.

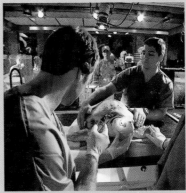

All but a tiny fraction of rescued Kemp's Ridleys are treated and released back into the wild. This was not possible for Scoot—her life-threatening injuries were too severe. A CAT scan in Scoot's medical records shows a collapsed lung; another scan shows how much the lung has healed under treatment at the center. The healing is not complete, however, and Scoot likely will never return to the Atlantic.

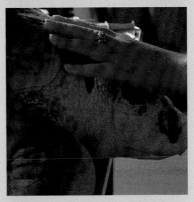

"Based on her condition, we don't think Scoot can be released into the wild again," says Weber. "But she's having a great life in our Giant Ocean Tank."

With any luck, Scoot's happy aquarium life may be a long one. In captivity, a turtle can live for as long as eighty years. Aging may create other prob-lems that the center will eventually have to monitor, but no one is certain. The staff is continually learning about the life cycles of turtles and other animals at the aquarium.

Artie the Hooded Seal

Turtles aren't the only rescued animals treated at the aquarium's medical center. For instance, a giant hooded seal found stranded on a beach near Boston once spent a few months at the aquarium. The staff named the

THE KEMP'S RIDLEY TURTLE IS A SPECIES IN SERIOUS DANGER OF EXTINCTION. ONLY A FEW THOUSAND OF THESE BUG-EYED REPTILES ARE LEFT, BUT THE AQUARIUM MEDICAL STAFF IS STRUGGLING TO SAVE AS MANY AS POSSIBLE FROM NATURAL AND HUMAN THREATS.

THIS HOODED SEAL ARRIVED AT
THE AQUARIUM AN EMACIATED
AND NEARLY LIFELESS BLOB.
AFTER MONTHS OF CARE AND
REHABILITATION, HE RETURNED
TO THE WILD.

emaciated male seal Artie. Completely bald and about half the normal weight for a male hooded seal, Artie was a very long way from his home waters near Greenland.

"He was extremely weak at the time," says Weber. "We gave him a physical exam and found that there wasn't a lot terribly wrong with him except that he had worms and parasites and he was extremely thin."

While treating Artie for parasites and bacterial infections, the staff tried to fatten him up, feeding him restaurant-quality herring, capelin, and mackerel. Adult hooded seals eat from twenty-five to thirty pounds of fish per day, so Artie was downing a lot of tasty seafood. Even so, it took almost four months for Artie to begin putting on weight and growing a fresh coat. Within five months Artie had overcome his infections and regained enough weight and strength to be released.

"It is unusual to rehabilitate animals of this size and nature," says Weber, noting that typically a hooded seal like Artie could weigh as much as 500 pounds. "That's a formidable animal."

In Artie's condition he probably would not have survived without human intervention, so Weber and his staff felt they had to help him or at least make the attempt. Apparently they succeeded. However, no one can say for sure how long he will live now that he has been returned to the wild.

"That's a question we often ask ourselves when we're doing rehabilitation," says Weber.

DEATH IS THE USUAL RESULT OF ENTANGLEMENT. IMPROVED FISHING EQUIPMENT AND TECHNIQUES COULD SAVE THE LIVES OF COUNTLESS SEA CREATURES.

Artie was the center's second adult hooded seal. The first, a female named Stephanie, was treated at the center in 1996. A tracking device on Stephanie showed that she did return to Greenland and was able to dive to an impressive depth of 2,000 feet. Based on satellite data from Stephanie, Weber feels confident that Artie will survive.

Fighting Extinction

The aquarium's rescue-and-release program is only part of a much broader conservation effort aimed at maintaining ocean species diversity. Much of this is directed at helping consumers make informed choices when they go to the market. What we buy and what we throw away can have a profound effect on life in the oceans. For instance, plastic is a wonderful material and indispensable to modern life, but in some forms it can kill.

Leatherback turtles, another species the aquarium is working to save, may be driven to extinction in part by plastic. In 1980 the worldwide leatherback population likely exceeded 115,000, but just fifteen years later their numbers had dropped to only 35,000. The threats facing leatherbacks are similar to those that endanger other species, but these turtles have a unique problem—plastic bags in the water. To the turtles the bags look just like jellyfish, their favorite food. Once a plastic bag has been ingested, it will clog the turtle's intestines, eventually killing the animal.

Making unwise choices about what seafood to put on the table may also diminish species diversity. Through a program called EcoSound, funded by two major foundations, a large seafood buyer, and several grocery chains, the aquarium is encouraging consumers to buy ocean-friendly seafood. The goal is to help buyers purchase seafood that is caught in environmentally responsible ways that do not damage the survival prospects of ocean species.

"The EcoSound Project is spreading," says Greg Stone, who notes that both consumers and retailers must be part of the effort. "Our EcoSound program is strategically designed. We're working not just with consumers but also with large wholesalers, helping them audit their seafood purchasing processes."

The EcoSound program likewise encourages fishermen and fish farmers to adopt environmentally sound practices. As Stone sees it, conservation helps maintain profits by preserving the source of that profit, namely the supply of quality seafood.

"Those in the seafood business realize that if they're not good ocean stewards, they may have no fish to sell in the future," says Stone.

AN ANIMAL STRUGGLES AFTER BECOMING ENTANGLED IN POORLY DESIGNED FISHING GEAR. LIKELY IT WILL NEVER BREAK FREE.

Watery Menagerie

Being a good ocean steward is what the New England Aquarium is all about, but this mission cannot be accomplished through conservation programs alone. Aquariums are, in essence, educational facilities. By exposing visitors to the rich and colorful diversity of life in the oceans, they hope to fire the public with a passion for conservation.

Putting on a good show for visitors is not always easy, however. While the aquarium exhibits may seem magical to visitors, a lot of legwork goes on behind the scenes to keep them filled with healthy animals. One challenge facing the aquarium that might never occur to visitors is that of finding appropriate mates for penguins. The aquarium's African penguins are part of a population of 700 scattered among more than fifty zoos and aquariums nationwide. The African penguin population in the wild is declining at a rapid pace, and this places pressure on zoos and aquariums to promote reproduction. The Association of Zoos and Aquaria regulates breeding of African penguins to maintain a genetically diverse population.

The difficult part is pairing penguins with sufficiently dissimilar genetic backgrounds. This usually requires moving penguins from one location to another. The penguin on loan is quarantined when it arrives, but once it passes a medical inspection, it is introduced to its mate. Observers will know that they have made a good match if the penguins start bowing and shaking their heads. The head bobbing and shaking,

CAPTIVE BREEDING PROGRAMS ARE HELPING PROTECT WILD POPULATIONS OF AFRICAN PENGUINS AND MANY OTHER THREATENED SPECIES.

accompanied by donkeylike brays, are part of the penguin courting ritual. If things go well, eggs will appear in late spring or early summer. After about forty days of incubation, there will be chicks. More than fifty penguin chicks have been hatched at the aquarium since it opened.

Sometimes aquarium animals breed with far too much success. The seahorses inhabiting the aquarium's Edge of the Sea and Living Links exhibits have produced hundreds of offspring—so many, in fact, that other homes had to be found for them.

Interestingly, it's the male seahorse that actually gives birth, and he can have as few as ten babies or as many as a thousand. The seahorse starts down the road to fatherhood by doing an elaborate dance with a female. Seahorses may swim together and even link tails during this courtship phase. Afterwards they swim to the surface and the male opens his pouch to allow the female to deposit her eggs inside. He fertilizes the eggs, and then the pouch serves as a womb until the small seahorses are ready for birth.

Even though seahorses don't look much like fish, they do have gills and fins. Experts have identified about forty different species of seahorses and estimate the number could be higher than one hundred. The Pacific seahorse, measuring about 12 inches in length, is the largest of these wondrous creatures; the smallest is less than 1 inch long. Other than by size, seahorse species are quite difficult to identify, as they can actually change colors like chameleons.

Like many other ocean species, seahorses are threatened, largely because of habitat destruction and because they are popular to collect and keep in home aquariums. Some cultures use dried and ground up seahorses to treat asthma, impotence, thyroid disorders, broken bones, and heart disease. The seahorse has been placed on the World Conservation Union's "red list" of threatened species.

One sea creature that visitors would certainly expect to find in a New England aquarium is the lobster. The aquarium has been conducting research into how to feed lobsters raised on farms, and occasionally a lobster takes up residence in an exhibit. Recently a fisherman gave the aquarium an extremely rare white lobster. Experts estimate that only one of every one hundred million lobsters is white. The ivory-colored lobster was placed in an exhibit and also became part of a research project on shell diseases.

FOR OBVIOUS REASONS CLOWNISH ROCKHOPPER PENGUINS ARE POPULAR WITH VISITORS.

COVERED WITH SCALY CALLOSITIES,
RIGHT WHALES ARE UGLY, BUT
THEIR EXTINCTION WOULD BE A
GREAT TRAGEDY.

Worldwide Aquarium

Research on lobsters, a commercially important species, may seem a natural, but the scientific work the New England Aquarium promotes extends far beyond the confines of the northeastern United States. The New Zealand Hector's dolphin, bluefin tuna, and African cichlid fish are among the far-flung species that receive the attention of aquarium researchers. Scientists in the aquarium's Edgerton Research Laboratory study habitats worldwide, and staff strive to identify conservation issues and raise public awareness. The aquarium often uses research findings to create exhibits.

"But we're not limited by the exhibits here at the aquarium," says Greg Stone. "We're limited only by the oceans and by the problems facing them. Unfortunately those problems are quite extensive, and we feel a responsibility to address them."

Researchers at the aquarium tackle a wide variety of topics, such as the effects of fishing, aquaculture, and a host of other human activities on ocean habitat. Some of this research has had a very positive effect. For instance, aquarium research in the Gulf of Maine has demonstrated that the use of acoustic devices on fishing nets reduces accidental deaths of porpoises.

"We feel an obligation to go out where the wild relatives of our aquarium animals live and perform conservation projects," says Stone. "The need has gotten great over the past ten or twenty years as the human footprint on the planet has expanded and reached into

A DIVER FEEDS FISH BROUGHT TO THE NEW ENGLAND AQUARIUM FROM DIVERSE HABITATS SCATTERED ACROSS THE GLOBE.

almost every part of the ocean. Aquariums have been changing to meet that need. Modern aquariums have really only been around for about thirty-five years, and they are still finding their appropriate roles in society. I think the New England Aquarium and a few others in the United States are identifying that role, are finding that battleground, if you will, by bringing their energies and resources to bear on solving the problems of our planet's oceans."

CHAPTER 3

At the end of Cannery Row in the old sardine-packinghouse district of Monterey, California, a window opens onto the sea.

Monterey Bay Aquarium

It is the Monterey Bay Aquarium, where visitors enjoy sweeping vistas of sparkling blue salt water. Defined by wave-swept rocks in the foreground, golden dunes along its eastern shores, and fog-shrouded mountains in the distance, the bay inspires many to pull out their cameras. But the real attraction here is not the scenery—this is a place for looking beneath the surface of things. Actually, the aquarium is not one window but many, both real and metaphoric, offering close and often eerily personal glimpses of a world far removed from our everyday experience and yet vital to our very existence.

Like most other aquariums, this one educates and entertains while encouraging a commitment to worldwide marine conservation, but the focus of the exhibits here is not planetary in scope. Rather, the Monterey Bay Aquarium showcases the habitats and sea life of one of the world's richest marine environments—Monterey Bay itself. Dropping from the tidal pools and beaches near sea level down

through a winding submarine canyon to a depth of more than 2 miles, the bay harbors an extraordinarily diverse population of sea plants and creatures ranging from simple, single-cell plankton to marine mammals, such as the whales and sea otters that are so popular with tourists.

The bay is especially rich in what some might mistakenly believe are less attractive creatures—jellyfish. A nearly endless variety and number of these diaphanous, long-tentacled predators drift to and fro with the great rivers of current that flow through the bay. The aquarium is justifiably famous for its jellyfish displays. Carefully lit to emphasize their beauty, the jellies seem more reflection than substance. Their parachute-like bodies constantly in motion, they create a sort of living, surrealist art. The jellyfish displays can mesmerize aquarium visitors, who often stand before them in awestruck wonder for minutes, even hours at a time.

Aquarist Chad Widmer manages the award-winning jellyfish exhibits at the aquarium. Part of his responsibility is to provide the jellyfish that go into the displays. Some of the jellies are grown at an in-house laboratory culture facility, but most of them come straight out of the bay. Widmer collects them. It's a job that he especially enjoys because it takes him out on the water.

Piloting a 14-foot Boston Whaler through waters that are sometimes calm but more often choppy, Widmer can reach one of several highly productive collection areas in just a few minutes. Most are located only a mile or so from shore, right in the aquarium's own watery backyard.

"There are three or four spots out here where jellyfish tend to accumulate," says Widmer, who has worked at the aquarium for more than six years. "It has to do with the direction of the swells and the way the wind blows."

Widmer looks here and there for a glassy slick or a patch of lightly disturbed water, signs that the jellyfishing may be good today. Collecting the jellies takes experience, an in-depth knowledge of the currents, and occasionally a bit of good luck. Having found a likely spot, Widmer tosses his net, gathers in some jellies, and carefully stores in plastic bags those likely to become part of an aquarium exhibit. Those that are not needed, he gently returns to the bay.

Usually when he goes collecting, Widmer has particular species in mind, for instance, so-called comb jellies or sea gooseberries, needed for one of the aquarium displays. When he is lucky, he finds them, but of course, he is not always lucky.

"I do have a shopping list," says Widmer. "But I learned long ago that it's really better to have an open-ended shopping list. If we can collect any jellies at all, that's terrific, because I'm certain we can always make use of them."

THE AQUARIUM IS TIGHTLY FOCUSED ON MONTEREY BAY, BEST KNOWN FOR ITS SEALS AND SEA OTTERS BUT EXTRAORDINARILY RICH IN OTHER MARINE SPECIES. AQUARIST CHAD WIDMER REGULARLY VENTURES OUT ONTO THE BAY TO GATHER SPECIMENS FOR AWARD-WINNING JELLYFISH EXHIBITS.

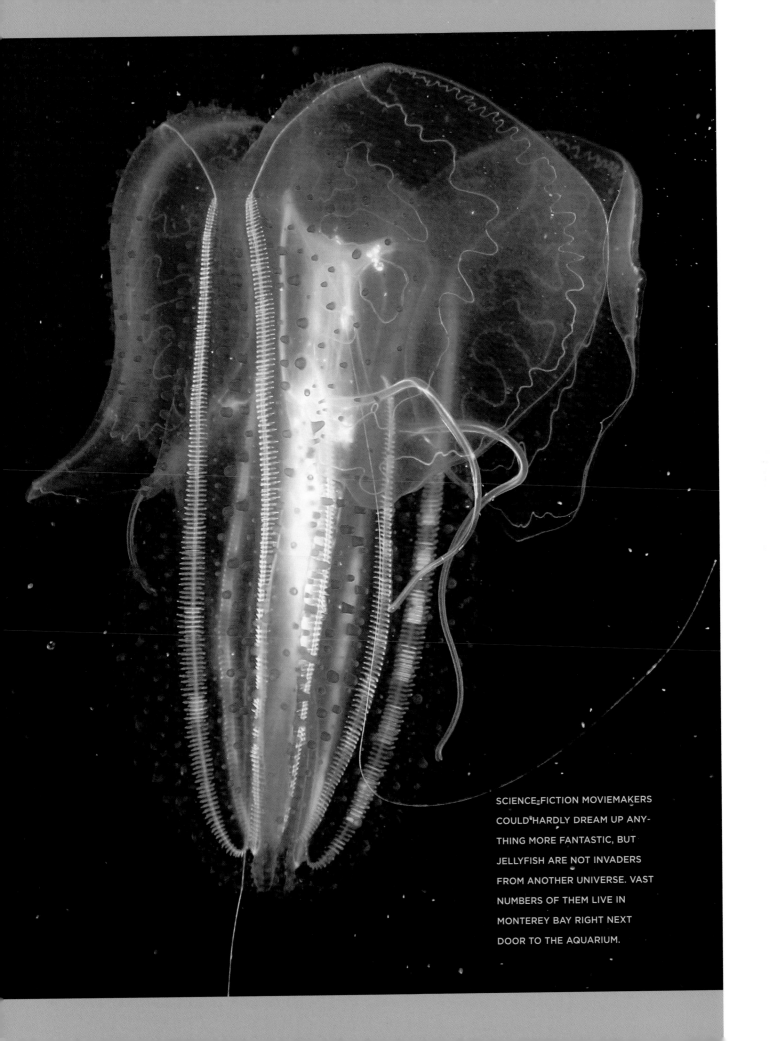

SCIENCE-FICTION MOVIEMAKERS
COULD HARDLY DREAM UP ANY-
THING MORE FANTASTIC, BUT
JELLYFISH ARE NOT INVADERS
FROM ANOTHER UNIVERSE. VAST
NUMBERS OF THEM LIVE IN
MONTEREY BAY RIGHT NEXT
DOOR TO THE AQUARIUM.

JELLIES COME IN AN ENDLESS
VARIETY OF SIZES, SHAPES,
AND COLORS.

Back on land, Widmer transfers his catch to a temporary home, one of many transparent storage tanks in the aquarium jellyfish laboratory. Eventually, the day's catch may end up in the Drifters Gallery, one of the aquarium's most dynamic display complex and one of the largest permanent collection of jellyfish in the United States.

Like the aquarium itself, Widmer works in partnership with Monterey Bay. He has found that he can depend on its life-generating waters to provide, if not precisely what he had planned for, then something that will do just as well—perhaps even better.

Widmer's approach is more than coincidentally in tune with that of Edward F. Ricketts, a marine biologist who lived and worked beside the bay several generations ago. Ricketts's eccentric ways and dedication to the bay were celebrated in the novel *Cannery Row*, written by his friend John Steinbeck. Ricketts operated the Pacific Biological Laboratory, where he collected and shipped specimens of marine life to classrooms, research biologists, and curiosity seekers around the world. Interestingly, Ricketts's lab was located immediately adjacent the old Hovden Cannery, which later became the site of the Monterey Bay Aquarium. Ricketts believed that the living abundance of Monterey Bay was worthy of celebration, and so did the founders of the aquarium.

"Monterey Bay was really the inspiration for the Monterey Bay Aquarium," says executive director Julie Packard. It was Packard's parents, David and Lucile Packard, who through a personal gift provided the money that made the aquarium possible. Since opening day, revenues from admission fees and membership dues, business sponsorships, and private donations have supported the aquarium, a nonprofit institution.

SEA NETTLE JELLIES SWIM IN AN INVERTED POSITION LIKE UPSIDE-DOWN PARACHUTES.

"Our mission is to inspire conservation of the oceans," says Packard. Many other aquariums pursue similar missions, but Packard notes that the Monterey Bay Aquarium differs from them in at least one key respect: "Our theme is the Monterey Bay. The idea is that you can tell all the stories the oceans have to tell based on this one place."

This bold concept—the notion that the world's oceans could be brought into clearer focus through the lens of the Monterey Bay—was perhaps first put forward by Edward Ricketts. During the 1970s, long after Ricketts was gone, the concept found renewed support among a group of marine biologists working at a latter-day Ricketts Lab, the Stanford University Hopkins Marine Station, located just west of Cannery Row. Together with members of the Packard family, they formed the Monterey Bay Aquarium Foundation in 1977. Seven years and some $55 million later, the aquarium was completed and opened to the public.

A Link to the Past

The need for a better understanding of our planet's inner space—the oceans—and for a commitment to ocean conservation is a motive linking the aquarium to Cannery Row and the history of Monterey. Some of that history is painful, for only about sixty years ago, Monterey Bay was the site of a maritime ecological disaster of immense proportion: the collapse of the California sardine fishery. Tim Thomas, the Monterey Maritime Museum historian, is familiar with this calamity.

"The sardine industry began around the turn of the twentieth century," says Thomas. "A. E. Booth, the father of the industry, had been in the salmon business up along the Sacramento River during the 1890s, but around 1895 he came to Monterey."

By the time Booth arrived, Monterey's fishing industry was already well established. Dating from the 1850s, when several families of Chinese fishermen established a small village just west of the city, it depended largely on squid and salmon. Booth found that he could make good money off the boatloads of salmon being landed at Monterey wharves, but he was soon convinced there were even greater profits to be made from sardines. The bay was teeming with massive schools of these small fish, and Booth believed that the public might develop a taste for them. With the help of immigrant Sicilian fishermen, who were familiar with the techniques necessary for netting sardines, and with a little clever marketing,

HISTORIAN TIM THOMAS SEES LINKS BETWEEN THE MODERN AQUARIUM AND MONTEREY'S DEFUNCT SARDINE INDUSTRY.

SARDINES LIKE THOSE IN THE
KELP FOREST TANK ONCE RAN
IN VAST SCHOOLS AND BENT
THE BACKS OF MONTEREY
FISHERMEN.

Booth launched a successful enterprise. His advertisements appeared in publications from coast to coast, even in the Sears & Roebuck catalog.

Booth's success attracted other investors, and by the end of World War I, there were nine large canneries in operation along what is now called Cannery Row. Scores, if not hundreds, of sardine boats crowded the wharves at Monterey, and nearly 400 Sicilian fishermen earned a living in the local industry. Within twenty years, the number of canneries had grown to nineteen, and they bustled day and night as an average 225,000 tons of sardines were pulled from the bay annually. Some said there were enough sardines coming out of the bay each year to fill trucks lined up hood-to-bumper all the way from Monterey to Sacramento and back again.

"It's important to remember that the majority of the sardines being netted out on the bay weren't going into cans," Thomas notes. "They were grinding them up for fish oil, fertilizer, and chicken feed."

The agricultural use of these cheap fish contributed to the drain on the sardine fishery, and following peak years in 1938 and 1939, catches began to decline. After World War II they dropped off precipitously—and just kept falling. Marine biologists had warned for years that the fishery could not indefinitely sustain catches of the sizes netted during the late 1930s. Sooner or later, overfishing, combined with such natural pressures on fish populations as cyclical changes in water temperature and associated disruptions in the food chain, would take a heavy toll on the once fabulously abundant sardine. It happened, and the booming Monterey sardine fishing and canning business slipped into a steady and irreversible decline. In 1972 the Hovden Cannery shut down, and the last of the large Monterey sardine operations was gone.

Exhibits at the Monterey Bay Aquarium recall the history of the Hovden Cannery and the sardine industry as a whole. Some of the Hovden boilers and other cannery equipment are preserved within the aquarium walls. A living tribute to the part commercial fishing played in the history of the Monterey Bay region can be found in front of the aquarium's spectacular Outer Bay wing. There, in an enormous circular tank, thousands of tiny silver anchovies swim round and round with an exuberant singleness of purpose that we humans are at pains to comprehend.

Bounty from the Bay

The ancestors of the little fish that enliven the circular tank at the entrance to the aquarium's Outer Bay wing might have ended up in cans to be dished out spoonful after oily spoonful as somebody's lunch, but that would be unlikely to happen today. The Monterey Bay canning industry vanished about half a century ago along with the vast schools of small fish that had made it possible. Gone, too, is the rough and tumble Cannery Row that John Steinbeck described in his poignant novels *Cannery Row* and *Sweet Thursday*.

As with all great literature, Steinbeck's novels were, in a sense, more real than reality itself. The stories he told and the themes he explored cut to the heart of the human experience, not just on Monterey Bay but anywhere. The Cannery Row of *Cannery Row* may never have existed at all, and if it did, it's gone forever.

"I think the Cannery Row we talk about today and that John Steinbeck wrote about in his wonderful book was something of a myth," says Thomas. "People come here looking for his Cannery Row, looking for Doc Ricketts, looking for Mac and the boys, and they don't find any of that."

What they do find is a Monterey that has made peace

WITH CATCHES SHARPLY REDUCED, MONTEREY'S ONCE-THRIVING PACKING INDUSTRY DECLINED. THE COLORFUL CANS AT RIGHT ARE MEMENTOS OF ITS HEYDAY.

NOWADAYS, THE LIVING THINGS IN MONTEREY BAY ARE MORE HIGHLY VALUED FOR THEIR BEAUTY AND SCIENTIFIC INTEREST THAN FOR THE PRICE THEY ARE LIKELY TO FETCH ON GROCERY STORE SHELVES.

with its past and discovered a new way to make money from the bay—lots of money. Tourism has replaced the fishing industry as the mainstay of the local economy. Visitors flock to the Monterey Peninsula, not just during the standard Memorial Day–to–Labor Day tourist season but year-round. They come to play golf beside the Pacific. Two of the peninsula's noble oceanside or "links" courses—Cypress Point and Pebble Beach—are consistently ranked among the finest in the world. They come to enjoy the breathtaking scenery. The famed 17-Mile Drive through Pebble Beach and Highway 1 through the Big Sur Country to the south of the peninsula offer enchanting vistas of a coastline so beautiful and gardenlike that it hardly seems real. And, of course, they come to experience the wonders of the Monterey Bay Aquarium.

A trip to the aquarium takes visitors about as close to the Monterey of Steinbeck and Ricketts as they are ever likely to get—and that's not very close. To reach the aquarium, most people park a few blocks away and walk through the Cannery Row district, but it is a very different place from the one Steinbeck wrote about during the 1940s. The old canneries have given way to restaurants, gift shops, wine-tasting

rooms, specialty stores, and inns. In a small park near the center of the district is a bronze statue of a weighty-eyed Steinbeck gazing out onto a street filled with tourists rather than cannery workers. Interestingly, the same natural phenomenon that brought the workers here also brings in the tourists—Monterey Bay.

Of Tourists and Sardines

No less beautiful than it is bountiful, the bay has long attracted travelers. It is easy to imagine that in the eighteenth century Padre Junipero Serra built California's most important mission in Carmel on the Monterey Peninsula because the area was so lovely. A well-known nineteenth-century visitor was author Robert Louis Stevenson, who arrived in California via the very first transcontinental passenger train and spent several idyllic weeks in Monterey. Some say he wrote part of *Treasure Island* while staying here.

LIKE HUMANS, SHARKS ENJOY SEAFOOD, SO THEY FREQUENT MONTEREY BAY WHERE PICK- INGS ARE PLENTIFUL.

THIS ORCA (KILLER WHALE)
IS ONLY A MODEL, BUT IT
SYMBOLIZES THE GREAT
DIVERSITY OF LIFE IN
MONTEREY BAY.

"Monterey has been a tourist community since at least 1880, when the Hotel del Monte was built," says Thomas.

Designed by architect Arthur Brown and completed in 1880, the grand, high-Victorian Hotel del Monte had hundreds of rooms and kept them filled. Guests delighted in carriage rides through the peninsula's tall pine forests along what would come to be known as 17-Mile Drive. There was no Pebble Beach or Cypress Point in those days, but golfers could take a turn on the local Del Monte eighteen-hole course, the first one built west of the Mississippi River. However, Monterey Bay itself was then, and remains today, the peninsula's biggest attraction. Visitors enjoyed the local beaches and the sun, when there was any—the bay is notoriously foggy—and they went for long walks along the rocky, wave-dashed shoreline just west of town. Perhaps they wondered what was out there beneath the bay's blue, sky-reflecting surface.

Among the things out there, of course, were great schools of pilchard, a variety of small herring, which about the turn of the twentieth century would begin to be netted in fantastic numbers and sold across the country as sardines. The rapid growth of the sardine industry quickly brought it into conflict with Monterey's tourist-oriented businesses, including the Hotel del Monte. The canneries were regarded as unsightly, smelly, and generally unattractive to visitors.

"The folks at the Hotel del Monte were very unhappy," says Thomas. "They were passing petitions around to stop the canneries from moving in along the waterfront. But the city of Monterey knew there was money to be made off the sardines, and so they compromised."

The city allowed the sardine canneries to be built and operate in Monterey as long as they were grouped together on the far western side of town, well away from the business and hotel district. That way, hotel guests would not be troubled by unsightly canneries or, unless the wind was blowing in the wrong direction, have their appetites spoiled by the unmistakable odor of the latest catch. In the end, Monterey's sardine and tourist industries managed to coexist. The canneries prospered, and so did the Hotel del Monte. The grand Victorian edifice had burned in 1887, but it was quickly rebuilt with a near twin of the original. The hotel burned again in 1924 and was rebuilt once more, this time in an art deco style more in keeping with the times.

Ironically, the fortunes of both the sardine industry and the hotel started to decline at about the same time. During the 1940s the canneries withered along with the mighty schools of pilchard that had once kept them humming. The hotel never fully recovered from the lean years of the Great Depression, and following World War II it was sold to the U.S. Navy for use as a postgraduate school. The old building still stands and remains a key part of the Navy school complex.

Even after the Hotel del Monte closed, tourism remained an important component of the local economy. Aside from the famed golf courses in nearby Pebble Beach, however, Monterey lacked a tourist attraction with the magnetism to rival that of the grand old hotel in its heyday. In 1984 that would change.

Beyond Cannery Row

All the while that fishermen and sardine canneries had been reaping the natural wealth of the bay, others had been studying it. The research that the self-educated Edward Ricketts had begun would later be continued by marine biologists with degrees from major universities.

"I studied marine biology at Stanford and spent many summers at Hopkins Marine Station," says Steve Webster, one of several young scientists who, together with members of the Packard family, helped found the Monterey Bay Aquarium. For many years Webster served as the aquarium's senior marine biologist. Now retired, he does volunteer work helping introduce aquarium visitors to the wonders of the deep.

During the 1970s, when Webster was making regular visits to Hopkins, the Stanford research station stood in uneasy proximity to the ruins left behind by Monterey's now-defunct sardine industry. Once-bustling Cannery Row was now a jumble of abandoned cannery buildings. One of them was right next door—the old Hovden Cannery, which in 1973 became the last on the Row to squelch its ovens and bolt its doors. Some at Stanford feared that the property

STEVE WEBSTER (LEFT) WAS ONE OF SEVERAL STANFORD UNIVERSITY MARINE SPECIALISTS WHO SAW THE MAKINGS OF A MODERN AQUARIUM IN THE OLD HOVDEN CANNERY.

UNDERWATER WINDOW CLEANERS

To duplicate and maintain complex underwater environments such as the one in its dramatic Kelp Forest, the Monterey Bay Aquarium nourishes them with fresh seawater. Every minute, thousands of gallons of water are pumped from the open bay into the enormous tanks containing the Kelp Forest and other exhibits. This provides the exhibits with an authentic appearance that few other aquariums could reproduce. They are, in essence, a living extension of the bay.

During the day the water is filtered so that visitors can enjoy a clear view of the plants and sea creatures, but at night unfiltered water flows through the exhibits. The raw seawater brings with it rich nutrients and plankton, as well as spores and larvae of plant and animal life that settle in the tanks and grow. While this enhances the displays, it also creates a problem. Anytime raw seawater comes in contact with a foreign surface such as a window or the inside of a pipe, algae and other growing things begin to accumulate.

Keeping the display windows clear and free of algae and barnacles is a hefty task, especially in the enormous Kelp Forest tank. Three times a week, teams of divers must wipe every square inch of the tank's acrylic windows with nylon-mesh cloths. Otherwise

THE AQUARIUM RELIES ON VOLUNTEER DIVERS TO KEEP ACRYLIC WINDOWS FREE OF BARNACLES AND ALGAE.

the windows would be virtually opaque in a matter of months. Missing even one scheduled cleaning may give barnacles a chance to settle and secrete their calcareous shells, with unfortunate results—the next time the windows are cleaned the shells will scratch the acrylic. The aquarium uses volunteers to handle this tedious though necessary task, but there is no shortage of willing divers. There are 150 names on the volunteer list.

---

would be sold and become the site of a large new hotel or industrial facility that could detract from the important research being done at Hopkins. To prevent this, the university bought the cannery.

"We became very familiar with the building," says Webster. "We often had our 'TGIF' get-togethers over in the cannery, and we'd ask ourselves what would be a good use for this old rusting building next door to the marine station. It was during one of those discussions that the word 'aquarium' first came up."

An aquarium! The idea made sense, and it took hold among the scientists and their associates at Hopkins. So, too, did the notion that the aquarium should focus exclusively on the colorful and complex marine life found in Monterey Bay, not coincidentally the same subject matter studied by the research station.

As it turned out, the concept also intrigued industrialist David Packard. As a teenager in 1929, Packard spent a month in the resort town of Pacific Grove not far from Cannery Row. Perhaps it was there that Packard developed what would become a lifelong fascination with the ocean and love for Monterey Bay. Packard later studied at Stanford and went on to help found the Hewlett-Packard Company, amassing an immense personal fortune along the way and becoming one of the nation's most generous philanthropists.

Presented with the aquarium proposal in 1977, Packard and his wife, Lucile—principals of the Packard Foundation—gave the project careful consideration. Would a nonprofit aquarium located in a small community the size of Monterey attract enough patrons to keep the doors open? The studies they had commissioned suggested the aquarium might succeed, so the Packards decided to provide the millions needed to demolish much of the old cannery, build the aquarium, and place it on a sound financial footing. Some might say the Packards had personal reasons for making this decision.

"It really was a Packard family project," says Webster. "Two of their daughters, Julie Packard and Nancy (Packard) Burnett, were trained as marine biologists on Monterey Bay."

In fact, Nancy Burnett worked as a biologist at Hopkins, and she was part of the small group of station researchers who came up with the idea for an aquarium in the first place. With the backing of David and Lucile Packard, she and several of her associates helped form their own separate nonprofit foundation to plan and run the new facility. Her sister Julie soon joined in the effort.

"Yes, the aquarium was a project of the Packard family," says Julie Packard, who has served as director of the aquarium for nearly twenty years. "My sister and some of her colleagues had the idea and got me involved, and our parents became very engaged in the subject matter. It really was something that gave us a lot of pleasure to create as a family, but the scope and scale of the place was more a reflection of my father's vision."

DIRECTOR JULIE PACKARD PLAYED A KEY ROLE IN THE SUCCESSFUL EFFORT TO ESTABLISH THE AQUARIUM DURING THE 1980S.

TOURISM HAS REPLACED SARDINES AS THE MAINSTAY OF CANNERY ROW. REBORN AS A WORLD-CLASS AQUARIUM, THE OLD HOVDEN CANNERY HAS NOT ALL TOGETHER FORGOTTEN ITS PACKINGHOUSE PAST.

Indeed, the aquarium project turned out to be a bigger undertaking than anyone, with the possible exception of David Packard himself, could have imagined. "Early on we were naive enough to think we might just freshen up the old cannery, and that would be the aquarium," says Webster. "But as soon as the engineers arrived and took one look at this building, they just sort of giggled at that thought. It was so dilapidated that it literally had to be torn down. Virtually all of what you see here today, except the boilers and the warehouse building where the offices are located, is new structure."

It took seven years to get the aquarium built, establish the exhibits, and open the doors to the public. And when they opened, would people come? Would they travel long distances to visit an aquarium so tightly focused on Monterey Bay, a tiny corner of the vast, interconnecting universe of oceans and seas that cover much of our planet?

Some might have thought that concentrating exclusively on the marine life of Monterey Bay was too risky, but the Packards and their associates didn't think so—and still don't. Webster thinks it was the right decision.

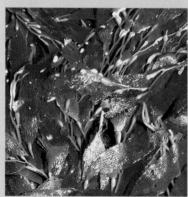

"Right offshore here you have the nation's largest national marine sanctuary," says Webster. "It's a remarkable coastal marine system that includes more species diversity—seaweeds, birds, mammals, fishes, and invertebrates—than you would find anywhere else."

Another concern was the relatively small population of Monterey Peninsula, only about 100,000. "No other major public aquarium is located in a community that small," says Webster. "We knew we would depend on tourism from San Francisco, Los Angeles, and the country at large. That's why our original estimates were conservative. We thought we might see 350,000 visitors our first year. Instead we had more than a million."

People came, and they would keep coming. They came because, from the first, they understood they were stepping into a mysterious and beautiful world such as they had never experienced in their lives—the world of the Monterey Bay.

Underwater Forest

California is known for its trees, the tall coastal redwoods and mighty mountain sequoias that stand among the largest living things on the planet, but its giant forests don't stop at water's edge. In the ocean just off California's rugged shores still greater forests grow. Among the most impressive of these are the huge beds of kelp found in or just outside the Monterey Bay Marine Sanctuary, the nation's largest protected offshore reserve.

Most aquariums stick to fish, sharks, turtles—anything that swims. Sea animals are popular with aquarium patrons and, one might think, more dramatic than exhibits that celebrate plants. Well, think again.

What some describe as the crown jewel of the Monterey Bay Aquarium is its enormous kelp tank. Located near the center of the aquarium's main building, the tank is a 28-foot-high blue-green wonder of gently undulating kelp. Sunlight streams down from the surface, which is open to the sky, while leopard sharks, sardines, and numerous other fishes glide between the kelp fronds. The tank offers a near-perfect re-creation of one of the planet's richest environments and one of Monterey Bay's most profound spectacles—a giant kelp forest.

"Giant kelp is a large brown algae that grows just off the coast of Monterey," says Julia Mariottini. A senior aquarist for the Monterey Bay Aquarium, Mariottini is a member of the Kelp Forest team that maintains the aquarium's remarkable kelp exhibit. "It creates a three-dimensional habitat essential for animals living on the surface of the ocean and living in midwater. It provides cover, refuge, and, for some animals, food as well."

LOCATED RIGHT ON THE WATER, THE AQUARIUM PROVIDES A COMPREHENSIVE VIEW OF MONTEREY BAY FROM ABOVE AND BELOW THE SURFACE. SENIOR AQUARIST JULIA MARIOTTINI SAYS THIS AQUARIUM WAS THE FIRST TO DISPLAY LARGE QUANTITIES OF LIVING GIANT KELP.

THE KELP FOREST EXHIBIT
PROVIDES AN EXPERIENCE
MUCH LIKE THAT OF DIVING
INTO THE BAY.

The kelp forests in Monterey Bay also serve as a playground for divers who arrive in the hundreds every weekend to explore them. The aquarium founders were all avid divers who wanted to share with aquarium visitors some of the joys and wonders they had experienced while diving in the bay. Foremost among these were the bay's vast kelp beds with their tall, swaying stalks and teeming sea life.

The Monterey Kelp Forest exhibit is unique in that it was the first to display live kelp in an artificial aquarium environment. "I believe there are some other institutions that now show live kelp," says Mariottini. "But this exhibit, which opened in 1984 along with the aquarium itself, was the first."

There were reasons no other aquarium had succeeded in establishing a living kelp exhibit, even if they tried. For one thing, kelps are very large plants, growing up to 60 feet or more from the ocean floor to just beneath the surface. For another, it is very difficult to keep the plants alive; they need plenty of sunlight, constant wave motion, and a continuous exchange of free-flowing, nutrient-rich water, which cannot be either too warm or too cold. In short, they require an environment exactly like the one that nurtures them offshore. Even nature is not good at maintaining such a delicately balanced environment. The range of the giant kelp is limited to the western coast of the Americas from California to Chile and some parts of

KELP FRONDS FLOAT ON THE SURFACE OF MONTEREY BAY, WHERE CONDITIONS ARE PERFECT FOR THIS BIG BROWN SEA PLANT.

southern Africa. Re-creating their habitat in a tank was no simple matter.

"Nobody had done a living kelp forest in an aquarium before, so we weren't real sure it would work," says Steve Webster. "Our colleagues said, 'Oh, nobody's done that; you probably can't do it, and even if you can, who wants to come see a bunch of brown seaweeds anyway?' Well, we knew better."

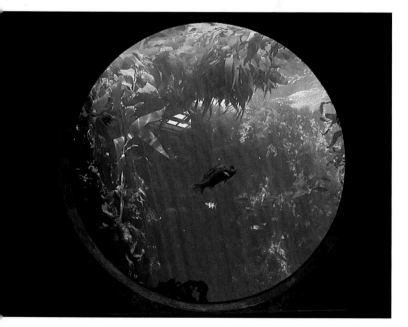

HUGE LENSLIKE WINDOWS MAKE A LIVING THEATER OF THE KELP FOREST EXHIBIT. MAGNIFIED SHARKS MAY APPEAR SHOCKINGLY CLOSE.

Since kelp thrived in the waters off the central California coast, it fit right into the new aquarium's Monterey Bay theme. David Packard encouraged the aquarium foundation to take a chance on these grand but surprisingly delicate giants. The aquarium founders set out to learn all they could about kelp, seeking the assistance of experts Mike Nuschel and Wheeler North, who were then engaged in kelp culture and reforestation efforts along the Southern California coast.

"Julie Packard went down to Southern California and learned to think like a kelp," says Webster. "And based on what she and the rest of us had learned, we decided that if we made the tank at least 28 feet deep, got lots of water moving through it, and opened it to the sky so that it got abundant sunlight, then we ought to be able to grow kelp."

The result was a three-story exhibit offering a diver's-eye view of the towering *Macrocytis pyrifera*, California's giant kelp. The plants in the exhibit grow up to 4 inches a day—a healthy rate, although only about half that of kelp in the bay. Hidden water jets in the exhibit's rockwork walls keep the water moving to help the kelp fronds absorb nutrients from the water.

The new aquarium had one important advantage—the relatively high quality of the water in Monterey Bay. There are no heavy industries or large metropolitan areas along the bay. Coastal cities and towns such as Monterey, Watsonville, and Santa Cruz carefully treat their sewage before it enters the bay. The largest source of pollution is the substantial runoff from farms in the Salinas Valley, but Monterey Bay is so large and its waters so well circulated that it can easily disperse these pollutants. As a result, the aquarium can safely pump water out of the bay directly into its exhibits. For the Kelp Forest exhibit, this is crucial.

"We're able to pump 2,000 gallons per minute, day and night, through the exhibits," says Webster. "It's this raw seawater, containing the spores of seaweeds and the larvae of invertebrates, that allows us to support real living communities like the kelp forest."

Fresh seawater was not the only requirement. Somehow the exhibit's designers had to find a way to replicate the incessant motion of the coastal waters where giant kelp grows naturally. To do this they installed a wave machine that produces a surge every few seconds, causing the kelp fronds to gently sway and enabling them to absorb the nutrients the plants need to survive. Aquarium visitors can't help noticing that the tank "breathes." In fact, its vertical motion can be mesmerizing. The fish, sharks, and other creatures in the tank move up, then down, up, then down again, continuously—but they themselves never seem to notice.

WHO IS LOOKING AT WHOM? THE KELP FOREST WINDOWS ARE SO TRANSPARENT THAT THE FISH SEEM LIKELY TO SWIM RIGHT THROUGH THEM.

Roly-poly Showmen

While the living kelp forest may be the Monterey Bay Aquarium's foremost achievement, the sea otter exhibit is its leading attraction. Looking ever so much like stuffed animals, the otters are especially appealing to children and even to retirement-age youngsters-at-heart, who vie with the kids for a glimpse at these roly-poly showmen. And the otters do put on a good show. They romp, rub, tumble, tussle, and roll just like the otters that can be seen along the rugged shores of the Monterey Peninsula, perhaps pounding the dickens out of a shellfish with a rock. However, these are not wild otters.

Since sea otters are a threatened species, no aquarist would consider capturing a wild otter for display in an exhibit. The aquarium's otters are mostly orphans that, as pups, somehow became separated from their mothers and were rescued. Having never learned the ways of their natural ocean habitat, they lack the skills they would need to survive outside the exhibit. Other aquarium otters have been injured so badly they can no longer survive in the ocean.

Otter survival has become a matter of intense concern for marine biologists and for nature lovers, who read with alarm newspaper articles suggesting that wild populations are once more in decline. Highly specialized marine mammals with peculiar habits and finicky appetites—they dine mostly on sea urchins, clams, and certain species of crab—sea otters may never have been numerous, but there were once far more of them than there are now.

Once ranging along the Northern Pacific rim from Japan to the Arctic and down the coast of North America as far south as Baja California, the world population of sea otters once may have numbered to a maximum of about 300,000. In California alone there were likely as many as 20,000. Unfortunately the otters' own lustrous pelts proved to be their worst enemies. Containing approximately a million hairs per square inch, they are the thickest coats known in nature and so lush that fur traders hunted the otters to the edge of extinction. Today the California population has recovered somewhat and hovers just over 2,000.

"Currently the population seems to have leveled off," says Michael Murray, a veterinarian with eighteen years' experience at the aquarium who specializes in sea otters. "The latest census suggests a population of between 2,000 and 2,500 otters. We're a little concerned that it's not continuing to grow."

Murray's concern is well founded. The otters' small numbers and limited range—extending along only about 150 miles of coast from Santa Cruz in the north to Santa Barbara in the south—make them highly vulnerable to oil spills, contagions, and other calamities. A single such disaster might push them over the brink to extinction.

ALTHOUGH ENDLESSLY FASCINATING, THE KELP FOREST IS NO MORE POPULAR THAN THE AQUARIUM SEA OTTER DISPLAY. THE FUZZY OTTERS PUT ON A GREAT SHOW JUST BY ACTING NATURALLY.

"Our patient is no longer the individual animal," says Murray. "It's the entire population. We're hopeful that we can save not just a few otters but the whole species."

The aquarium maintains a pair of programs aimed at lending these marvelous creatures a helping hand. The first and less visible of the two is the Sea Otter Research and Conservation Program. The program operates behind the scenes to support research efforts focused on free-ranging or wild sea otters. Many important questions must be answered. Are their numbers declining, and if so, why? What, if anything, can be done to save them from extinction?

A key component of this program involves the rescue of orphaned, sick, injured, or stranded otters. The distressed otters are captured and brought back to the aquarium for treatment and rehabilitation. If possible, the otters will be returned to the wild. Those that cannot be sent back into their native environment may very well make a significant contribution to their species through a second aquarium program.

SEA OTTERS ARE FREQUENTLY SEEN FEEDING OFF THE ROCKY SHORES OF THE MONTEREY PENINSULA.

SEA OTTER PUPS STICK CLOSE TO THEIR MOTHERS. WHEN ORPHANED THEIR ONLY CHANCE MAY BE RESCUE BY HUMANS.

"That's the husbandry and education program," says Murray. "The sea otters we have on public display help teach people about the oceans. Hopefully, they can stimulate and inspire people to conserve."

The otters may be their own most influential ambassadors. At the aquarium they frolic in their 45,000-gallon tank to the delight of the crowds that gather at windows located both above and below the water's surface. It is easy to understand why, in the minds of many, they have come to symbolize the Monterey Bay Aquarium.

"The sea otters definitely have become an icon species for the aquarium, and there are a couple of reasons for that," says Laura McKinnon, senior sea otter aquarist. With five years' experience at the aquarium, McKinnon leads the team that maintains the sea otter exhibit. "First of all, they're native to our Monterey Bay region. Also, we're the only rehabilitation center for southern sea otters. If you see an otter in any public aquarium, it likely came through our rehabilitation program and, unfortunately, didn't graduate, didn't make it back into the wild."

The otters work hard to earn their popularity, mostly just by being them-selves. Although the tank is not like the habitat they knew or would have known in the wild, McKinnon and the other aquarists try to make their environment as stimulating as possible. Feedings—the otters are fed four times a day—provide excellent opportunities to encourage natural behav-iors. Otters have voracious appetites, and in the wild they eat shellfish and other seafood equal to about 25 percent of their body weight every day. Because their food is more nutritious, aquarium otters eat a little less, about 15 percent of their body weight. Even so, they go at it with gusto. The aquarium feeds them fish fillets, squid, shrimp, and chopped clams—about $12,000 worth per year per otter. Some of the food is stuffed into shell-like toys, a tactic that causes them to pound, prod, jiggle, and oth-erwise behave just as they would in the wild.

"The neat thing about otters is they're always busy, always doing some-thing," says McKinnon. "As members of the weasel family, they're naturally curious, always exploring their environment. Also they're very endearing. They have a very cute, furry, cuddly appearance that makes you want to just come up and hug them."

However, it would be a mistake to regard sea otters as a sort of oceango-ing teddy bear. Typically they avoid contact with humans, preferring to keep to themselves. If approached they may become aggressive and can inflict severe bites. They are, after all, creatures of the wild with wills and ways that are entirely their own. Still, these furry sea creatures that make so many of us laugh also have valuable lessons to teach.

"They're not necessarily separate from you and me," says McKinnon. "They might live in the ocean and we on land, but we're still connected. The things we do directly affect the lives of otters out in the wild. Here at the aquarium we try to get across that message—the need for conserva-tion of the oceans and of the species that thrive there. Of course that includes sea otters."

Plunging into the Deep Blue

The message that our destinies as humans are inescapably bound to the ocean and to the life in it is easier to convey with playful otters than with the creatures of the deep. During the 1990s, however, the aquarium decided it was time to reach for the outer margins of Monterey Bay, some 60 miles from shore. An astounding array of new exhibits of unprecedented scale were planned to give visitors a sampling of life at the edge of the precipice, where the shallower waters of the bay drop down into a canyon more than 10,000 feet deep. Completed and opened to the public in 1996, the Outer Bay wing cost some $57 million, more than had been spent to establish the aquarium itself about a dozen years earlier.

LAURA MCKINNON LEADS THE TEAM THAT MAINTAINS THE OTTER EXHIBIT. SHE AND OTHERS ATTEMPT TO REHABILITATE RESCUED OTTERS AND RETURN THEM TO THE WILD. WHEN THAT IS NOT POSSIBLE, THE OTTERS BECOME PERMANENT AQUARIUM RESIDENTS.

A SWIRLING TANK OF
ANCHOVIES WELCOMES VISI-
TORS TO THE OUTER BAY
GALLERY, WHERE THEY'LL FIND
SHARKS, JELLIES, AND OTHER
DENIZENS OF THE REGION'S
DEEPEST WATERS.

While the new wing retains the "cannery-style" architectural feeling of the original aquarium buildings, it carries the concept of the glass-windowed tank into a whole new realm. For instance, the circular overhead anchovy tank near the entrance provides fresh meaning to the notion of having one's head swim. Up to 3,000 anchovies keep the tank in constant, silvery motion.

At the far end of the wing is its showpiece, one of the largest windows in the world. Some 54 feet long, 15 feet wide, and 13 inches thick, this acrylic masterpiece weighs 78,000 pounds. Of course the exhibit behind the window is the true cause for celebration. It is a 90-foot-long, 35-foot-deep tank filled with a million gallons of seawater. This indoor sea is alive with mighty ocean predators—some graceful, others menacing, and all beautiful. Hammerhead and soupfin sharks share the tank with turtles and tuna, some of them giants weighing more than 300 pounds.

A MASSIVE ACRYLIC WINDOW, WIDER AND TALLER THAN A THEATER SCREEN, IMMERSES VISITORS IN THE WONDERS OF THE OUTER BAY.

THE MILLION-GALLON OUTER BAY TANK IS SO LARGE THAT THE SHARKS, TUNA, TURTLES, AND OTHER LARGE SEA CREATURES THAT LIVE IN IT MAY BE UNAWARE THEY ARE IN CAPTIVITY.

"Few other aquariums in the world have attempted to exhibit the giant tunas, which are used to a world without boundaries," says Julie Packard. "Here the tuna have the room they need."

Living Art

In the Outer Bay wing between the anchovies and the tuna lie the jellyfish exhibits, or Drifters Gallery. Here visitors may come face to face with boundaries not of space but rather of the spirit. Unlike otters, jellyfish are not playful and do not look cuddly. Unlike sharks and tuna, they do not display strength and determination—qualities we humans can admire. Yet the jellies are surprisingly attractive. More than with any other set of aquarium exhibits, visitors coming out of the jellyfish gallery are likely to say, "I've never seen anything to match that in my entire life." And they are right.

"Jellies are not something you see every day," says aquarist Chad Widmer. "They're unusual. They're unique. You can go to any pet store and buy a goldfish, but you won't find a jellyfish there."

TENNESSEE AQUARIUM

The Monterey Bay Aquarium concentrates on a single stretch of life-rich salt water along the California coast. Chattanooga's Tennessee Aquarium has found a much different but nonetheless effective way to narrow its focus—by celebrating freshwater habitats. When the first of its two main display buildings opened to the public in 1992, nearly all of its exhibits were devoted to life in ponds, swamps, and rivers, mostly those of the American South. Dubbed "River Journey" it transported visitors from the South's Appalachian highlands and down winding rivers all the way to the seacoast.

THESE JUVENILE ALLIGATORS MIGHT BE FOUND IN ANY SOUTHERN SWAMP. INSTEAD THEY ARE PART OF THE RIVER JOURNEY ADVENTURE.

THE TENNESSEE AQUARIUM'S RIVER JOURNEY BUILDING CELEBRATES FRESHWATER ANIMALS LIKE THESE RIVER COOTERS.

During their journey, visitors encountered animals seldom seen in an aquarium—creatures much more likely to be seen in a backcountry ditch. Some were quite rare, while others were downright familiar—or at least they were to Southerners. Displayed in and around tanks and pools containing 400,000 gallons of fresh water were catfish and bass, green tree frogs and snapping turtles, rat snakes and moccasins, and of course alligators, but these critters were no less wondrous for being native to the region. Aquarium planners may have thought that Southerners had forgotten how marvelous their own wetlands could be, and it seems they guessed right. Visitors have flocked to the 130,000-square-foot, $40 million River Journey building beside the Tennessee River and have delighted in the thousands of reptiles, amphibians, and fish on display there.

In 2005 the aquarium launched a second adventure and opened up a whole different world of possibilities with its new 60,000-square-foot Ocean Journey building. A ten-story structure with tanks holding a total of 700,000 gallons of salt water, Ocean Journey has much in common with aquariums that emphasize sharks, rays, tropical fish, dolphins, and other showy marine animals. Rather than shatter the aquarium's former focus, however, the addition complements it. Together, the River Journey and Ocean Journey experiences serve as reminders that the earth's fresh and saltwater environments are inevitably linked, just as we are to them.

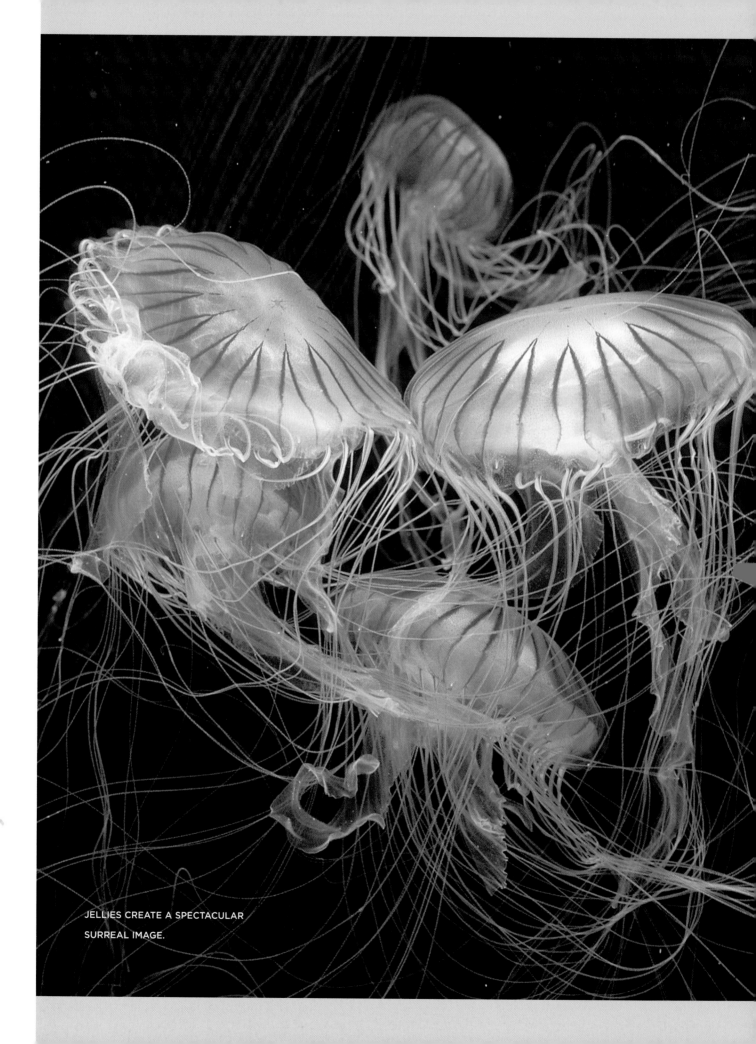

JELLIES CREATE A SPECTACULAR
SURREAL IMAGE.

Although these creatures make up a sizable fraction of the living matter on our planet, most people know very little about them. Much of what we have heard about them is erroneous. As children we were warned that jellyfish sting and might even kill an unwary wader. The truth is that only a few of the countless varieties of jellyfish are likely to sting, and even those are rarely dangerous.

"Very few jellies can actually injure you," says Widmer. "But a lot of people are afraid of them. They just haven't seen jellies very often. Actually jellies are good animals."

Widmer, on the other hand, sees jellyfish all the time; he might be said to be on intimate terms with them. Supplying the grand Drifters Gallery at the aquarium takes more jellyfish than can be caught out in the bay. To keep the exhibits full, Widmer grows jellyfish in a special laboratory overflowing with jars, some of them spread out into the hallways. The transparent containers are alive with one or another variety of the jellyfish Widmer cultures for the aquarium.

"It's really important to know how to culture your own jellies," says Widmer. "That way you don't have to rely on collectors, who can charge you an arm and a leg—as much as $170 for one big moon jelly." Still, there are challenges involved in growing them.

ALTHOUGH JUST AS MUCH ALIVE AS ANY HUMAN, JELLIES ARE MADE UP ALMOST ENTIRELY OF WATER.

The aquarium displays as many as nineteen different species of jellyfish—moons, crystals, combs, egg yolks, sea nettles, and more than a dozen others. The jellyfish found only in Monterey Bay are grouped together on the second floor of the Outer Bay wing. Those that can be found in the bay as well as throughout the world are displayed on the first floor. Each species requires a different culturing process

DESPITE THEIR OTHERWORLDLY APPEARANCE, JELLIES ARE KIN TO EVERY LIVING THING ON OUR PLANET. STEVE WEBSTER AND OTHER AQUARIUM SPOKESPERSONS NEVER TIRE OF MAKING THIS POINT.

KEEPING AQUARIUM TANKS FILLED WITH HEALTHY JELLIES REQUIRES ENORMOUS EFFORT AND A SPECIAL LAB FOR CULTURING THESE DELICATE ANIMALS.

and a different sort of care, but Widmer understands the needs of each. He also knows that his efforts will be well rewarded by the expressions on the faces of visitors when they enter the Drifters Gallery.

"Jellyfish are great," says Widmer. "They're very colorful, very good-looking animals. They've also got that beautiful, rhythmic, sort of relaxing pulsing motion that just draws people into the exhibit."

The popularity of the Drifters Gallery and the wonder it engenders may be the essence of the Monterey Bay Aquarium and what, for more than twenty years, it has sought to accomplish. With its jellyfish exhibits the aquarium brings us face to face with the strangest of strangers, creatures totally unfamiliar that, in fact, live in vast numbers just a few steps from where the surf reaches up to erase our footsteps from the beach. Some have speculated that if aliens from another world should land on our planet, they might attempt to communicate with us not with words but with music. Jellyfish—these alien beings from the depths of our own native earth—speak to us through visual art and in doing so stretch our consciousness beyond the limits of what we thought possible.

A LUMINOUS RESIDENT OF
THE DRIFTERS GALLERY.

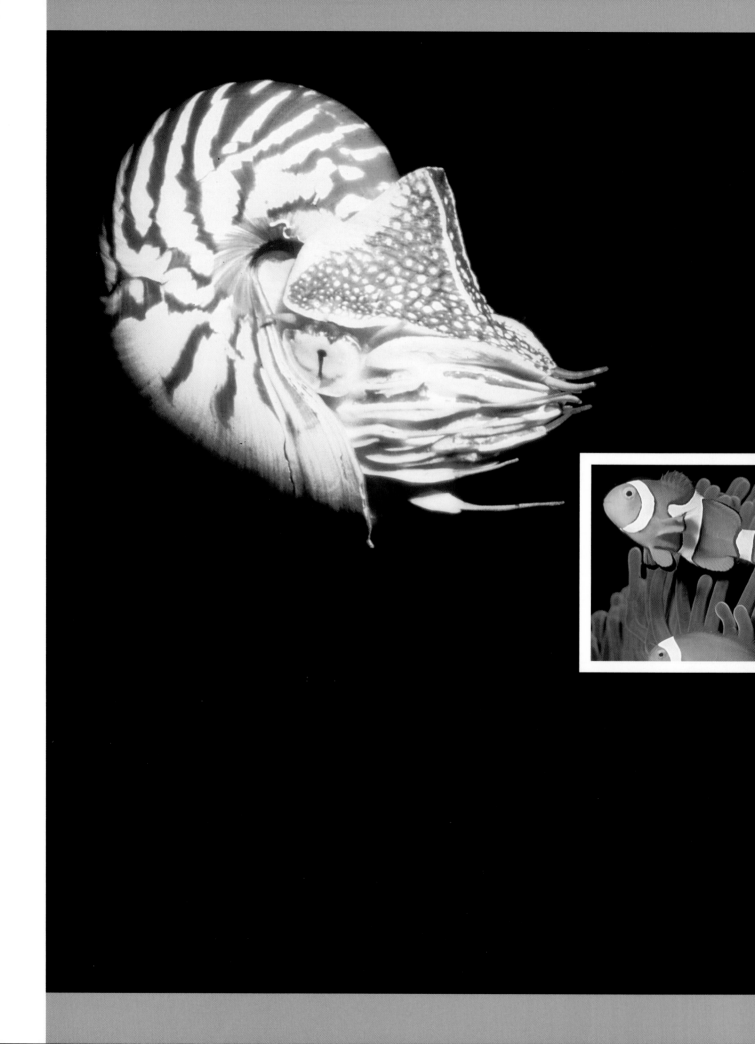

CHAPTER 4

A short distance from Oahu's famed Diamond Head and Waikiki, two underwater worlds wait to be discovered.

Waikiki Aquarium

  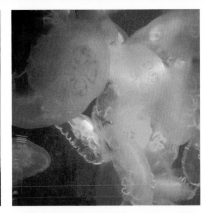 

The first is a massive sunlit reef located just off the shores of Queen Kapiolani Park. Teeming with life and splashed in a rainbow of colors, it protects the Hawaiian coast by holding the pounding Pacific surf at bay. The second is the equally bright and colorful Waikiki Aquarium, which might be considered both a figurative and literal extension of the reef.

Ironically, while Hawaii is America's fiftieth and youngest state, the Waikiki Aquarium is a venerable oldster. Founded in 1904, and operated as part of the University of Hawaii since 1919, it is the third oldest public aquarium in the United States. When its doors opened more than a century ago, few Americans had ever set foot in an aquarium or even heard of one.

THE WAIKIKI AQUARIUM LOOKS DIFFERENT TODAY THAN IT DID A CENTURY AGO WHEN IT STOOD AT THE END OF A HONOLULU TROLLEY LINE.

The aquarium was established as something of an afterthought, an outlying destination meant to coax paying passengers onto Honolulu's brand-new trolley system. The Hawaiian companies that operated the system built the small but well-designed aquarium to give passengers a reason to ride their trolleys all the way out to the end of the line.

At first considered more of a curiosity than a full-blown attraction, the little aquarium nonetheless attracted more than its share of visitors, who kept the trolleys busy shuttling them out to see the rare tropical fish in its well-conceived and up-to-date exhibits. Among those who made the trip and had a look were famous orator William Jennings Bryan and author Jack London.

"The aquarium was literally located at the end of the streetcar line," says Andrew Rossiter, director of the aquarium. "But I like to refer to it now as the beginning of a journey."

Rossiter's leg of the journey began recently. In 2004, the aquarium's centennial year, he became only the fifth director in its entire century-long history. Continuity is an important theme in the story of the Waikiki Aquarium, and Rossiter believes today's aquarium has much in

LOCATED IN A PLACE MANY CALL PARADISE, THE AQUARIUM HAS AN OPEN, SUNNY CHARACTER WELL SUITED TO ITS ISLAND HOME.

common with its predecessor, which was located just down the road from the present facility. The aquarium is still relatively small—and still known for the diversity and beauty of its tightly focused exhibits. Except for the fact that the streetcars are gone, the aquarium and its mission haven't changed much either.

Says Rossiter, "We want to entertain and educate people, and hopefully send them home with a respect and thirst for knowledge about the marine life around these islands."

There are challenges aplenty for Rossiter and his experienced staff. For instance, the aquarium must compete with a wide range of other destinations and activities for the time and money of potential visitors.

"We've got Diamond Head literally a four-minute drive away, and we're about a fifteen-minute walk from Waikiki," says Rossiter. "There are lots of alternative sources of entertainment, so we have to carefully define our niche."

The aquarium faces its most significant competition from the Hawaiian Islands themselves. The allure of their lush climate and spectacular scenery is legendary. A true tropical paradise pairing lush rain forests against dry mountain slopes carpeted with wildflowers, rugged volcanic peaks against gently rolling farmland planted in pineapple and sugar cane, sparkling high country rivulets against towering

DIRECTOR ANDREW ROSSITER BELIEVES THE AQUARIUM BENEFITS FROM ITS LONG HISTORY.

Pacific rollers, and rose-colored reefs against golden beaches, the islands are rich in splendid scenic contrasts.

"Obviously, there are plenty of natural wonders to see and enjoy around here," Rossiter says, but he is quick to add that visitors will find many of those same wonders at the aquarium. More important, they'll learn what lies beneath the scenery and what can be done to protect it.

"They're going to see almost all the habitats found around these islands," he says. "There's huge diversity, and visitors will be able to see and enjoy it without even getting wet. What's more, if they come to the aquarium before they go scuba diving or snorkeling, they'll be better prepared for what they'll see once they get in the water."

Islands of Life

Located almost 2,200 miles from North America, the nearest large landmass, the Hawaiian archipelago is the most isolated island chain on the planet. There are plants and animals both on the islands and in the surrounding waters that can be found nowhere else on earth. People who come to Hawaii expect to encounter the unexpected, and they are not disappointed.

The Waikiki Aquarium is, like the islands themselves, very much a place apart. Visitors are surprised by what they see here and by the very deep impression it makes on them. Many consider the time they spend wandering among its artful, sunlit exhibits unlike any previous aquarium experience.

THE AQUARIUM COMPETES WITH OTHER ISLAND ATTRACTIONS SUCH AS THE BEACH RESORTS ON WAIKIKI.

NATURAL SETTINGS, BRIGHT
SUNLIGHT, AND LIVING CORAL
COMBINE TO CREATE BEAUTIFUL
AQUARIUM EXHIBITS.

OPEN TANKS CONSTANTLY BATHED BY ARTIFICIAL TIDAL SURGES ENABLE THE AQUARIUM TO GROW ITS OWN CORAL.

A TINY FOREST OF TWIG CORAL IN A WAIKIKI DISPLAY.

takes full advantage of one of Hawaii's most abundant resources—sunshine.

"Ours is the only aquarium in the United States, and one of very few in the world, that makes extensive use of natural sunlight to illuminate its exhibits," says Rossiter. "This is one of the reasons we do so well with our corals and invertebrates."

During the evening or on one of Hawaii's rare cloudy days, the aquarium employs artificial lighting, but whenever possible, exhibits rely on the same warm orb that brightens and brings life to the islands, the ocean, and the rest of the planet—the sun. Its light sparkling on the surface of the tanks visually opens them and makes them seem larger. It also adds an authenticity to the exhibits that likely could be achieved in no other way.

"The first impression visitors get is that we're small," says Rossiter. "But once they take a careful look at our tanks, they realize that we focus on quality instead of quantity. It's not just the fish in the exhibits—and we have more than 2,500 species—but it's also the backgrounds. Almost everything in our tanks is alive, including the coral. People are amazed by the beauty and color of the living coral, since what they've usually seen before is the dead white skeleton, the rock you often see in gift shops."

Unlike the exhibits at most other aquariums, very little of what visitors see in a Waikiki Aquarium display is artificial. This is true in part because the aquarium

The use of natural light is more than just for looks, however. Without it, many of the exhibits could not exist at all, for they are chock-full of living coral. Including at least 117 species of stony coral and 18 species of soft coral, the aquarium's live coral collection is the largest and most diverse in the nation.

Coral is a fitting specialty for the Waikiki Aquarium, since coral reefs like the one just off the shores of Kapiolani Park are key to the very existence of the Hawaiian Islands. "Coral is the reason we're here today," says Rossiter. "If it weren't for our coral reefs, much of this land would have washed away long ago, and a lot of the marine life wouldn't be here either."

SOME MAY THINK CORALS ARE PLANTS, BUT NOT SO. WELL-INTERPRETED EXHIBITS MAKE IT CLEAR THAT THESE REEF BUILDERS ARE PART OF THE ANIMAL KINGDOM—THEY JUST DON'T MOVE AROUND A LOT.

YOUNG AQUARIUM VISITORS LEARN ABOUT THE MANY DIF-FERENT TYPES OF CORAL AND THE STONY STRUCTURES THEY LEAVE BEHIND WHEN THEY DIE.

In part because coral is both integral and essential to the Hawaiian environment, the aquarium focuses on coral conservation and operates a highly productive coral farm. "We started our coral propagation program more than twenty years ago," says Rossiter. "Now we send corals to aquariums all over the world. If aquariums don't go out and collect their own coral, it reduces damage to natural reefs."

To educate visitors about coral, the aquarium has created a multimedia exhibit called Corals Are Alive! It includes living exhibits, models, touch-screen interactive displays, and murals that focus on corals as animals. The exhibit highlights the aquarium's role in coral reef conservation while explaining the importance of reefs to life in the Hawaiian Islands—and to the planet.

More than a century ago the Waikiki Aquarium embraced the task of acquainting the public with the marvels of the ocean and the creatures it nurtures. Like with many other aquariums, however, that mission has evolved over the years to include research and conservation. Waikiki was one of the first public aquariums to perform ocean research; conservation is a more recent, but nonetheless important, emphasis. Naturally the aquarium's conservation efforts are focused largely on Hawaiian environments and species.

Monks of the Sea

One native Hawaiian species of particular interest to the aquarium and its visitors is the monk seal. Like too many other marine species, the monk seal is in serious jeopardy. Only a few scattered colonies of Hawaiian monk seals remain, mostly around the atolls and small islands that extend approximately 1,200 miles to the northwest of Kauai. Two of the threatened seals live at the Waikiki Aquarium, where they help inform the public by symbolizing the plight of their own kind as well as other troubled marine species.

"They're a big favorite with visitors," says Rossiter. "We try to use their popularity to promote a conservation message."

The playful seals are a treat perhaps even more rare than visitors imagine. Extremely scarce in the wild, they are wary of humans and practically never seen in captivity. "We were the first to put them on display," says Rossiter. "Even today, we're one of only two places in the world where you can see monk seals on exhibit."

Marine mammal specialist Stephanie Vlachos feeds and trains monk seals. On most days this entertaining process is open to the public. The

AS THIS MONK SEAL MAKES CLEAR, SOME AQUARIUM RESIDENTS ARE MUCH LIVELIER—AND NOISIER—THAN OTHERS.

better trained and friendlier of the two seals is a male named Nukaou, which in the Hawaiian language means "sleek swimmer." Nukaou came to the aquarium from Laysan Island when he was about three years old. Now twenty-four years old, Nukaou is no longer a youngster. Since monk seals live only about thirty years, he is well past middle age but, even so, remains quite active.

Vlachos fondly refers to Nukaou as "Nuka," and it is easy to tell that the seal has learned to trust his trainer. "We have a blue-and-white fishing float we use as a target," says Vlachos. "The seals have been trained to touch it, and Nuka knows that wherever the target goes he follows."

As is the case at most public aquariums, the seal training done at Waikiki is not for show but rather to make it easier to care for the animals. A well-trained seal is more likely to be cooperative when it requires urgent medical attention or routine procedures such as blood work or mouth exams.

"A mouth exam is voluntary for the seals," says Vlachos. "Nuka has been trained to participate by opening his mouth on cue rather than us having to open it for him. That way we can check his teeth, gums, and tongue and look for anything out of the ordinary."

MARINE MAMMAL SPECIALIST STEPHANIE VLACHOS MANAGES THE CARE AND FEEDING OF THE AQUARIUM'S RARE MONK SEALS.

Training also facilitates research that may benefit the species in the wild. Vlachos points out that a better understanding of monk seal biology, behavior, physiology, and thermoregulation may help save the species from extinction.

"The Hawaiian monk seal is a very endangered endemic species," says Vlachos. "Fewer than 1,400 monk seals are left."

VLACHOS EXAMINES NUKAOU'S MOUTH AS HE OBLIGINGLY COOPERATES WITH A HUGE YAWN. NUKAOU AND HIS FRIEND MAKA HAVE LIVED AT THE WAIKIKI AQUARIUM SINCE THEY WERE PUPS.

Species described as endemic are unique to a given region and believed to have evolved there. In the case of the monk seal, that region is the Hawaiian Islands. Hawaii's only other endemic mammal is a type of tree bat, which is also endangered.

Monk seal research often involves careful monitoring of food intake and body weight, which in an adult animal can reach more than 600 pounds. Scientists are anxious to learn more about fluctuations in weight of the seals and the thickness of their blubber. They hope this will shed light on causes for the steady decline in monk seal numbers. The population is growing smaller by about 5 percent each year, a rate the species cannot sustain for long. Some researchers speculate that malnourishment of pups and juveniles may be partly responsible for this alarming trend.

Waikiki's second monk seal, Maka, was only three weeks old when he was abandoned on a beach and left to fend for himself. Since monk seals typically nurse for six weeks, Maka would surely have starved if he hadn't been rescued by caring humans. A few years younger than Nukaou, Maka has been with the aquarium for more than twenty years.

While Maka survived his brush with death by starvation, many monk seals do not survive encounters with other hazards. Some lose their constant hide-and-seek competition with natural predators and become a meal for sharks. Others drown or starve after becoming entangled in fishing gear. Still others die from accidental ingestion of debris left in the water or on beaches by humans.

"To understand the severity of the marine debris problem, people need only take a stroll down the beach," says Vlachos. Beaches in Hawaii and elsewhere are often littered with discarded cans, bottles, and bits of plastic that have washed ashore with the tides or been left on the sand by careless picnickers. Such refuse can be deadly for many types of marine life, including seals.

Even the presence of humans in a sensitive area can be harmful to the seals. "Human encroachment on beaches is disturbing for moms with pups on those beaches," says Vlachos. "Seal mothers like their privacy. They want peace and quiet, and they want their pups protected."

A monk seal's ideal world almost certainly would exclude humans. Vlachos knows she must work hard to make her interactions with the seals as positive

MONK SEALS ARE A SEVERELY THREATENED SPECIES. ONLY ABOUT 1,400 REMAIN.

and helpful as possible. In the wild, a relationship like the one she enjoys with the aquarium monk seals would be impossible. "Probably monk seals got their name because they're a very solitary species," she says.

Other than their penchant for solitude, the behavior of Hawaiian monk seals in some ways resembles that of typical island visitors. Tourists tend to start their day with some activity but end up lounging on the beach during the afternoon. After a few hours of rest and relaxation, their evenings are filled with feverish activity, the difference being that while tourists are out seeking entertainment, monk seals are hunting and foraging. They may dive to depths of 1,650 feet hunting for food, which might include reef fish, octopus, or lobsters.

Nukaou and Maka do not live lonely lives like their wild relatives. Instead they are the stars of the show. "Having the monk seals at the aquarium is a great way to educate the public on a species they probably don't know about," Vlachos says. "Likely they would never see these seals in the wild."

TROPICAL FISH, AQUATIC
PLANTS, CORAL, AND GIANT
CLAMS—EVERYTHING IN THIS
BARRIER REEF EXHIBIT IS ALIVE.

Hunters on the Reef

Monk seals in the wild are vulnerable to predation by sharks. Neither the Waikiki Aquarium nor the scientists who conduct the aquarium's research take sides in the age-old game of predator versus prey, which is one of nature's key balancing mechanisms. Not surprisingly, however, the aquarium houses these natural enemies in separate exhibits.

Sharks are a featured predator of Hunters on the Reef, a 35,000-gallon exhibit that is also home to jacks, groupers, snappers, stingrays, and a variety of other animals. Interpretive panels provide an introduction to shark biology, research, conservation, and the safety procedures employed when working with them. Visitors learn that sharks and other large predators are neither wanton killers nor mindless eating machines. Rather they are efficient hunters that play a leading role in nature's drama.

While visitors do not get to see the predation process in action, they get close enough to some of the predators. Although of relatively modest size, the 3- or 4-foot-long blacktip reef and zebra sharks in the Hunters on the Reef exhibit are still very impressive.

In the wild, blacktip reef sharks swim constantly above the reef, while zebra sharks might be found resting on the seafloor; they demonstrate these same behaviors in their highly realistic aquarium environment.

Hunters on the Reef became a primary feature of the aquarium following renovations in the early 1990s. The tank includes a natural-looking seascape sculpted in concrete to resemble those parts of the reef typically patrolled by big predators. There are plenty of crevices and holes where smaller fish can find shelter or slip out of the way of danger. Real lava boulders and reef rocks placed on local coral sands provide a realistic seafloor.

Sharks aren't the only hunters in the exhibit, which also features the open-ocean stingray, rarely seen in captivity, as well as sleek, silvery jacks and stocky, bottom-dwelling groupers. The exhibit gives visitors two views of the sharks and other marine life inside the tank. One window brings visitors close to the action; the other is a hemispherical bubble that lets them feel as though they are stepping inside the tank. From either window, visitors can watch staff members feed the predators with squid and fish three times a day. Because the predators are kept well fed, they don't eat other animals in the exhibit.

REEFS SERVE AS A HUNTING GROUND FOR PREDATORS SUCH AS THIS BLUEFIN TREVALLY, AT LEFT. CONSTANTLY IN SEARCH OF PREY, THE BLACKTIP REEF SHARK (RIGHT) IS A TIRELESS HUNTER.

The Predator's Sting

In addition to placing dramatic exhibits such as Hunters on the Reef before the public, the aquarium pursues active ocean research, some of which carries staff members far out onto the Hawaiian reefs. The shark research program is headed by curator Jerry Crow, whose primary responsibilities are the care of all the animals at the aquarium. Crow, a world-renowned shark expert, studies their distribution, reproductive biology, and diet, which in the case of tiger sharks sometimes includes monk seals. Crow's research is not limited to sharks, however. Stingrays are abundant in the waters surrounding the Hawaiian Islands, and on any given day Crow or other aquarium staff may be working with them.

Stingrays caught in nearby Kaneohe Bay are placed in a holding tank at the aquarium, where Crow and his associates take measurements,

FITTED WITH A SMALL TRANSMITTER, THIS STINGRAY WILL BE RELEASED INTO THE WILD SO RESEARCHERS CAN MONITOR ITS MOVEMENTS.

Crow tries to minimize handling the stingrays he works with. Usually the rays remain at the aquarium for no more than a week before being released back into the wild. The goal is to keep the stingrays in as natural a condition as possible. That's better for the stingrays, of course, but it's also better for researchers, who want the animals to behave normally in their home environments while their movements and feeding habits are being monitored.

"That's one thing we're really careful about," says Crow. "We try to make it all as noninvasive and painless as possible."

The process may, however, be painful to the researchers, unless they take care to avoid the venomous spine or barb located near the end of the stingray's tail, which can deliver a rather nasty sting to the unwary. An expert at handling the rays, Crow is unfazed—and usually unstung—by their barbs. "They really are gentle creatures," he says, "and so majestic in the water."

Although they are not necessarily endangered as a species, the brown stingrays common in Hawaiian waters are found elsewhere only in the seas off Taiwan. "Their range may extend farther than that, since we don't know a lot about them," says Crow.

determine the animals' age and sex, and place tiny transmitters on their backs. After the stingrays are released, the transmitters help researchers monitor their movements.

Each stingray is assigned a specific code, and its transmissions are received and recorded twenty-four hours a day by one or another of nine monitors placed on the bottom of the bay. If a stingray with a transmitter passes near a monitor, its code number is recorded along with the time of day.

"These bottom monitors help us get the movement pattern without having to be physically out there all the time studying the animal," says Crow. "Over time, the information we get from the monitors shows us how these animals move about and use the bay."

The information will guide future conservation efforts. "If you're going to set aside an area for protection, you need to know how much room the stingrays need," says Crow. "It's also important to know what these animals are feeding on and where. There is a large food web out there in Kaneohe Bay, and we don't fully understand how each of the animals fits into it."

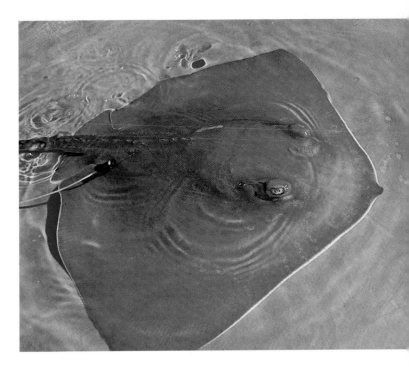

AQUARIUM RESEARCH CONTINUES TO SHED LIGHT ON THE BROWN STINGRAY, A CREATURE THAT SPENDS MUCH OF ITS TIME IN MURKY WATERS.

THE UNMISTAKABLE SHAPE OF ITS HEAD AND SNOUT, USED TO SIPHON TINY BRINE SHRIMP AND OTHER PREY, EARNED THE SEAHORSE ITS NAME.

BREEDING SEAHORSES AT SCRIPPS

Just as the Waikiki Aquarium is widely known for its coral propagation, the Birch Aquarium near San Diego has earned recognition for breeding an even more unlikely creature—the seahorse. Part of the Scripps Institution of Oceanography on the University of California–San Diego campus in La Jolla, the Birch Aquarium has long made a specialty of seahorses. Exhibits provide visitors with close-up views of these elusive and mysterious fish, which have nothing in common with horses but the shape of their heads.

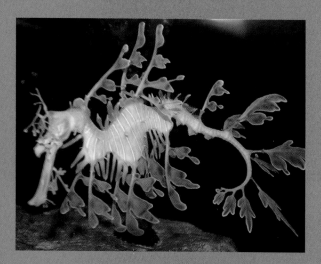

A RELATIVE OF THE SEAHORSE, THE LEAFY SEA DRAGON IS FESTOONED WITH TWIGLIKE APPENDAGES THAT PROVIDE EXCELLENT CAMOUFLAGE.

The Birch Aquarium began to focus on seahorses years ago, and during the 1990s the Birch introduced something new to the aquarium world—a large-scale seahorse breeding program. The idea was to raise enough seahorses to populate the aquarium's own jumbo-size seahorse exhibit and then, if the experiment went well, raise adult seahorses in numbers sufficient to supply other aquariums. The aquarium hoped in this way to reduce the pressure placed on wild populations by collectors.

The undertaking proved more complicated than one might expect. Aquarium experts set up a nursery room with forty-gallon tanks for adult seahorses, smaller ones for the juveniles, and a separate culturing tank for growing the tiny brine shrimp the seahorses

THE WEEDY SEA DRAGON IS ANOTHER SEAHORSELIKE ANIMAL EQUIPPED WITH BIZARRE CAMOUFLAGE.

eat. Seahorse hatchlings must start feeding within a few hours after they are born, and they require live shrimp so small that they are practically microscopic. This meant that the keepers had to breed the seahorses and shrimp simultaneously. It was no simple task, but after a shaky start the aquarium produced its first hatchlings on Thanksgiving Day 1994.

Since that time, the aquarium has been hatching seahorses on a regular basis and raising them to adulthood. So far the aquarium has shipped nearly 1,500 live seahorses to forty-five display facilities around the world, and the techniques developed here are now being used by other aquariums to propagate their own seahorses.

CAPTIVE STINGRAYS AWAIT EXAMINATION BY CROW AND OTHER MEMBERS OF THE AQUARIUM RESEARCH STAFF.

"One of the challenges facing us is to figure out how much they move around."

One reason so little is known about the brown stingray may be because it lives in murky waters, where its dark coloring provides excellent camouflage. "A lot of people in Hawaii don't even know we have stingrays in Kaneohe Bay," says Crow, "but they're quite abundant even though they can't easily be seen. There are literally hundreds of them out there in the bay at any given time."

Through research, Crow hopes to clear up some of the mysteries concerning stingray movements and habits. At the same time, the research may reveal vital information on Kaneohe Bay. It is believed that stingrays, hammerhead sharks, and many other species use the bay's protected waters as a nursery.

"The bay is a unique environment where stingrays come to pup," says Crow. "It's a natural birthing ground, offering protection from large predators such as tiger and Galapagos sharks that otherwise might feed on these animals and their young."

Crow thinks the young stingrays remain in the bay until they have grown to adult size and then move farther from shore. The bay is ideal for stingrays, since it offers "patcheries," small areas of reef crowded with the tiny fish and shrimp on which they feed.

Many-Chambered Nautilus

Researchers at the Waikiki Aquarium are also working to unlock the secrets of one of the South Pacific's most mysterious creatures, the chambered nautilus. It is a poorly known species and, unfortunately, a species in decline.

"We've found out a lot about the chambered nautilus in recent years, but a lot more still needs to be

ALAN NELSON IS HELPING UNLOCK SECRETS OF THE CHAMBERED NAUTILUS, A CREATURE THAT HAS EXISTED SINCE THE TIME OF THE DINOSAURS.

THE RECENTLY HATCHED NAU-
TILUS AT TOP CAME INTO THE
WORLD WITH EYES OPEN, BUT
THEY DETECT ONLY THE PRES-
ENCE OR ABSENCE OF LIGHT. A
CHAMBERED NAUTILUS HATCH-
LING REPRESENTS A BIG VIC-
TORY FOR THE AQUARIUM
BREEDING PROGRAM.

learned," says research associate Alan Nelson. Having joined the
aquarium staff more than twenty years ago while still a student at the
University of Hawaii, Nelson handles much of the feeding and nutri-
tional work with resident animals. He is particularly interested in the
chambered nautilus.

"They are fascinating animals," says Nelson. "People have always been
fascinated by their intricate and beautiful shells, and in time scientists
started wondering what the rest of the animal was like."

A chambered nautilus occupies a coiled shell divided into many separate compartments or chambers. The animal lives in the outermost
section; the inner chambers are filled with gas, which helps the nautilus
maintain its balance in the water. As the nautilus grows, its body moves
forward in the enlarged shell and produces a wall to seal off older
chambers.

These strange creatures live at depths of a thousand feet or more and
have features well suited to their extreme, high-pressure environment.
They have a primitive eye with no lens. The eye is basically a pore
capable only of distinguishing between light and dark. Tentacles
extend from the front of the shell surrounding the animal's mouth.
Below that a rolled tube or siphon squirts jets of water to move the
nautilus up, down, or sideways. Overall it's a simple biological design—
and an extraordinarily successful one. The chambered nautilus has
existed for a long time indeed.

"They have been around for hundreds of millions of years," says Nelson. "But people have only recently started studying them."

Described as living fossils by scientists, the chambered nautilus, or creatures much like it, has inhabited our planet's oceans for more than 400 million years, since before the time of the dinosaurs. Some wonder how much longer that lengthy record of survival can run, however, for although not much is known about these deep-ocean dwellers, at least one thing *is* known—their numbers are decreasing. This may be because collectors prize the nautilus's remarkable shell.

"The shells are beautiful, and that is part of the problem," says Nelson. "People are actually trapping these animals, pulling them up, and killing them just to get their shells."

Nelson advises conscientious collectors to avoid chambered nautilus shells. "They shouldn't buy chambered nautilus shells or have them on their mantelpieces," he says. "They're much too valuable to us all as living animals."

Another factor in the worldwide decline in chambered nautilus numbers may be their limited range. They are found only in certain regions such as the Indian Ocean and the tropical South Pacific. This makes them more vulnerable to loss of habitat than other more-widespread animals.

Since the chambered nautilus is not found in the Hawaiian Islands at all, those now housed at the aquarium were brought in from Palau, American Samoa, or Fiji. Two of these animals are on display in the aquarium's Jet Set exhibit; another four are kept away from public view for breeding and research purposes.

Much of the research effort at the aquarium focuses on propagation of marine species, including the chambered nautilus. Establishing a successful breeding program for the nautilus required a considerable amount of study in the wild. After extensive field research, aquarium scientists were able to build tanks that could duplicate the chilly temperatures and other rigorous environmental conditions of the nautilus's native habitat. The next step was getting them to reproduce, and the Waikiki Aquarium was among the first in the world to accomplish this. It was no easy trick.

To build a base of knowledge on the biology and reproductive habits of the chambered nautilus, aquarium researchers placed sonic transmitters on animals trapped near Palau. Able to track nautilus movements over time, scientists learned that they keep to the lightless deep during the day and then rise to a depth of about 300 feet at night. More important, researchers discovered that the nautilus lays eggs at shallow depths on rocks or coral.

"Once we understood their behavior and embryology, we started getting egg production," says Nelson.

The aquarium now has chambered nautilus hatchlings on display. In

SOFT TENTACLES PROTRUDE FROM THE NAUTILUS SHELL (TOP), GUIDING FOOD TO THE CREATURE'S MOUTH (TOP CENTER). ALTHOUGH THE NAUTILUS SWIMS (LOWER CENTER) AND SPENDS MOST OF ITS TIME AT EXTREME DEPTHS, ITS EGGS (BOTTOM) ARE LAID IN THE SHALLOWS.

appearance at least, they are miniature replicas of their parents. "Hopefully, through our research we can keep the program going," says Nelson. "Maybe we can get them up to full adult size and actually have them breed to produce a captive population."

Only in Hawaii

Although Waikiki's chambered nautilus exhibit is extremely unusual, other displays here are even more so. Some contain species that cannot be seen in any other aquarium.

"We've got a lot of rare Hawaiian fishes you won't see exhibited anywhere else," says aquarium biologist Charles Delbeek. "For example, masked angel fish are found only in Hawaii, and we are the only aquarium in the world to display them."

Another rare Waikiki Aquarium resident is the flamboyant cuttlefish, a native of Japanese waters. "We're the only aquarium outside Japan that displays them," says Delbeek. "We also have bearded armorheads from Japan, the only ones on exhibit in the United States."

A highly unusual Australian native has also found its way into a Waikiki Aquarium exhibit. A relative of pipefishes and seahorses, this strange-looking Aussie is called a leafy sea dragon. Looking nothing at all like a fish, the sea dragon intrigues visitors with its distinctive tubular jaw that opens rapidly to suck in prey and its bony plates that sheath its body in an armorlike casing. As they glide through the water, these small finned creatures very much resemble leaves. They can be so inconspicuous that they are often hard to distinguish from vegetation.

Leafy sea dragons live for only about seven years, but they make good use of their time by growing at a prodigious rate. Starting life at about three-quarters of an inch in length, they often end it nearly thirty times longer. Since the wild population of leafy sea dragons is protected under Australian law, the aquarium's specimens had to be raised in an aquaculture facility.

Although not unique either to the Waikiki Aquarium or to Hawaii, the aquarium's giant clams are nonetheless extraordinary. "These clams came from a mariculture facility in Palau," says Delbeek. "We received the larger of the two in 1982, when it was five years old and about the size of your fist. Today it is twenty-seven years old, and weighs 167 pounds."

THE LEAFY SEA DRAGON IS A NATIVE OF AUSTRALIA, WHERE IT BENEFITS FROM PROTECTED STATUS.

HOME AQUARIUM OWNERS
CANNOT HELP BUT ENVY THE
AMAZING VARIETY AND COLOR
ON DISPLAY IN WAIKIKI TANKS.

GIANT CLAMS DON'T PUT ON MUCH OF A SHOW, BUT THEY ARE NONETHELESS FASCINATING TO CHILDREN. PROBABLY THE OLDEST CLAMS IN CAPTIVITY, THESE GIANTS HAVE LIVED AT THE WAIKIKI AQUARIUM FOR OVER A QUARTER CENTURY. ONE WEIGHS MORE THAN 165 POUNDS.

The other big clam arrived one year after the first. "It was only about the size of your thumbnail, but by 2002 it weighed eighty-nine pounds," says Delbeek. "We believe these are probably the oldest clams in captivity anywhere in the world; they're certainly the largest."

Among some peoples, the giant clam has an undeserved reputation as a killer likely to snap off the leg or even the head of an incautious diver. This is a myth, for they are about as gentle as any creature on earth. They don't eat people, and their shells don't snap shut as though powered by steel springs. Instead,

UNLIKE THE AQUARIUM'S MORE COLORFUL AND SHOWY TROPICAL FISH, THE CUTTLEFISH AT LEFT IS NO THING OF BEAUTY. WAIKIKI'S BEARDED ARMORHEADS (RIGHT) ARE AMONG THE FEW ON DISPLAY OUTSIDE JAPAN.

DEAN SPENCER SUPERVISES
THE EDGE OF THE REEF, A
POPULAR WAIKIKI EXHIBIT
FEATURING NATIVE HAWAIIAN
SPECIES SUCH AS THE POT-
TER'S ANGEL AT TOP.

when threatened they slowly close their shells for self-protection. Divers and even small fish are much too large for a giant clam to eat, and the clams at the aquarium have never been fed anything except sunlight. For nutrition they filter plankton from the water. Experts estimate that the aquarium's clams could live another fifty years and reach weights of 600 pounds or more.

At the Edge of the Reef

Many of the aquarium's native Hawaiian species can be seen in its popular Edge of the Reef exhibit, which re-creates a stretch of island shore and features life from waters surrounding the Hawaiian Islands. Waikiki was among the first aquariums to place special focus on local ocean habitats. Others, such as the Monterey Bay Aquarium in California, have followed Waikiki's lead, creating exhibits that not only feature local species but also, like Edge of the Reef, in many ways are actually part of the environment that nurtures them.

THE REEF-DWELLING FROGFISH HAS AN UNENVIABLE FACE SOMEWHAT LIKE THAT OF A DRAGON IN A CHINESE NEW YEAR'S CELEBRATION.

Included in the Edge of the Reef are coastal plants, sand dunes, and rocky tide pools identical to those found along the Hawaiian shore. To mimic wave action, the shallow pools receive a surge of water every few minutes. Beyond the pools, there is a reef alive with cauliflower, finger, rice, brown lobe, and yellow lobe corals, just like those seen in Kaneohe Bay. Darting here and there along the reef are some of Hawaii's most colorful fish.

Coral reef fishes tend to be very brightly colored. Experts speculate that bright colors and intricate patterns help reef fish recognize their own kind among the thousands of other species that are part of their habitat. Some types of reef fish change colors and patterns two or three times during their lifetime.

"The fish and invertebrates in Edge of the Reef are endemic, meaning they are from here in Hawaii," says education associate Dean Spencer. Spencer supervises the Edge of the Reef exhibit, which has been in place for almost twenty years, and he considers the exhibit a tool for teaching valuable lessons about the importance of conservation.

"Conservation is our primary educational focus," says Spencer. "We have school and community programs that convey our conservation message."

PRICKLY PROTRUSIONS HELP PROTECT THE REEF LOBSTER (LEFT) AND HAWAIIAN TURKEYFISH (RIGHT) FROM PREDATORS.

A FOREST OF CORAL STALKS MAKES A PERFECT HOME FOR TROPICAL FISH. THIS IMPRESSIVE CORAL ARRAY WAS CULTURED AT THE AQUARIUM.

Classes held at the aquarium or out along the Hawaiian shore promote a better understanding of the ocean as well as economic and cultural issues related to conservation. The Edge of the Reef exhibit is itself a classroom of sorts, as aquarium staff members take the time to talk with visitors about conservation. "It helps to get the word out that ocean reefs are being damaged," says Spencer. "We want to replenish those damaged reefs."

Coral Farmers

If anything sets Waikiki apart from other aquariums, it is coral. Exhibits here contain an abundance of real, living coral—a spectacle that few visitors have seen elsewhere. Most other aquariums don't display live coral, at least not in the impressive quantities found at Waikiki, and for good reason. It is extremely difficult and expensive to acquire real coral and then keep it alive.

LIVING CORAL BEDS RESEMBLE COLORFUL GARDENS WITH MANY DIFFERENT TYPES OF SHRUBS AND FLOWERING PLANTS BUT ARE COMPOSED ENTIRELY OF ANIMAL LIFE.

THE WORLD'S CORAL REEFS ARE IN TROUBLE

Key links in the chain of ocean life, coral reefs are a vital component of our planetary ecosystem. Home to more than 4,000 species of fish and countless other creatures, they provide shelter for nearly 25 percent of all living things in the sea while breaking the force of ocean waves that otherwise would overwhelm fragile atolls and wash away vast stretches of beach. And yet, these ancient, nurturing structures and the tiny animals that built them up over the eons are in serious trouble.

Scientists believe that more than 10 percent of the world's coral reefs have been destroyed and another 16 percent severely damaged. Harm comes to reefs in a variety of ways. Heavy silting caused by widespread deforestation or dredging to create channels for ships has destroyed some reefs; unwise fishing practices have devastated others. But rising ocean temperatures represent the greatest threat.

Live coral thrives within a narrow range of temperatures. If the water gets too hot, the corals will die and the reefs they grew on will rapidly deteriorate. In recent decades meteorologists have noticed a steady rise in ocean temperatures likely caused by manmade global warming. During the 1998 El Niño "weather event," temperatures in the Pacific reached record highs, and coral reefs throughout the ocean's tropical regions showed signs of bleaching. High temperatures destroy the colorful algae inside the coral, causing it to turn white, or bleach. Since the coral depends on the algae for much of its sustenance, it too begins to die. Unless these trends are reversed and the threats to coral reduced, some scientists estimate that as much as one-third of the earth's coral reefs will be lost within the next thirty years.

SOME CORAL BEDS SUFFER FROM BLEACHING LIKELY CAUSED BY WATER TEMPERATURE INCREASES RELATED TO GLOBAL WARMING.

STALKS OF FINGER CORAL GROW IN A PROPAGATION TANK. IN TIME THIS CORAL WILL FIND ITS WAY INTO AN AQUARIUM DISPLAY.

"We use live corals in every exhibit," says Charles Delbeek. "Many other aquariums use fake coral, so that's what people are expecting to see. We take pains to point out to people that the colorful corals in our exhibits are actually alive."

Once people discover that coral is not dead stone but rather a living creature—a surprise to many—they next want to know how corals grow. They can learn this at the aquarium coral farm, which doubles as an exhibit. Corals begin as a single polyp but divide quickly, eventually forming large colonies. The aquarium gives visitors a chance to watch this process in action by placing small pieces of live coral in front of research cameras. The propagation of the coral can be witnessed either on a screen at the exhibit or on the aquarium's Web site.

Seeing corals move and propagate can be an eye-opener, especially for those who think of coral as lifeless rock or perhaps some sort of plant. Actually, corals are animals that in certain ways behave like plants. In fact, corals rely on plants—algae known as *zooxanthellae*—to keep them alive. The algae live inside the coral tissue, converting sunlight into energy by way of photosynthesis and thereby nourishing the host.

"They're like plants in that they require light to grow well," says Delbeek. "The corals easiest to keep here at the aquarium are the ones that need lots of light."

Because of the sunlight streaming into its coral tanks and other exhibits, the aquarium is able to grow a wide variety of healthy corals. "There's a great deal of variation between coral species in different parts of the world. We can grow most of those species here and provide them to researchers and scientists who need large quantities of a certain type of coral."

The Waikiki Aquarium's intimate association with coral began years ago, when a few fragments of exotic South Pacific coral were brought in from Fiji. These were used to establish a live coral exhibit, the first of its kind in the United States. Then, with the help of additional shipments of Fiji coral, the aquarium took a step that would eventually change the way corals are displayed and perceived around the world. A special tank was set up in the back of the aquarium for coral propagation. To create an environment similar to that in the corals' natural habitat, the tank was fitted with a surge device that provided a repetitive swell much as tides and waves would in the wild. The corals thrived, and the initial propagation unit proved so productive that several more tanks were soon added.

The aquarium now grows seventy-five separate species of coral typical of those found on reefs not

A PROPAGATION TANK AT THE WAIKIKI AQUARIUM CORAL FARM.

CORAL BEDS DELIGHT THE EYE
WITH A RIOT OF SHAPE, FORM,
AND COLOR.

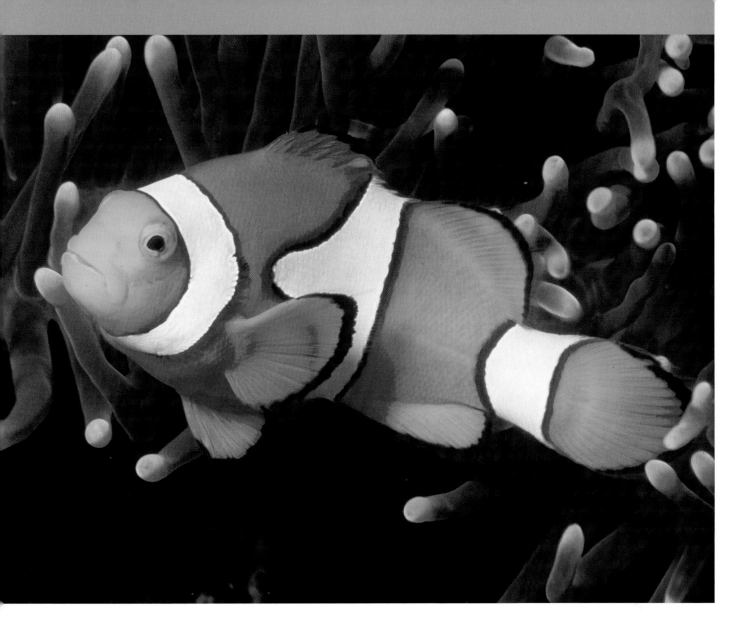

just in the Hawaiian Islands but also in Fiji, Palau, Guam, the Solomon Islands, and throughout the Pacific. Aquarium staff members bring back small fragments of living reef from these and a wide variety of other locations, and they are cultured at the aquarium coral farm. Other aquariums use these cultured corals in their exhibits rather than gathering their specimens in the wild.

"We've sent out as many as 2,600 pieces of coral since that time," says Delbeek, "and today there probably isn't an aquarium in the United States that doesn't display at least some of our corals."

The aquarium's pioneering propagation efforts received a boost from a number of resources the Hawaiian Islands possess in abundance— clean, low-nutrient water, warm temperatures, and bright sunlight. It also helped that coral propagation turned out to be a relatively simple process.

"We basically take a head of coral, break off small branches, and mount them onto a rock," Delbeek says. "Afterward the coral just grows. It's similar to growing new plants from plant cuttings."

THERE MAY BE NO MORE COL-
ORFUL ENVIRONMENT THAN
THAT OF A CORAL REEF. HERE
A BRIGHTLY PAINTED CLOWN-
FISH PEEKS OUT FROM A
BLANKET OF SEA ANEMONE.

BIZARRE BUT BEAUTIFUL, THE *TRIDACNA MAXIMA* IS ONE OF THE MANY TYPES OF CLAMS THAT POPULATE REEFS. OUR NATION'S PUBLIC AQUARIUMS CELEBRATE THE GREAT DIVERSITY OF LIFE FOUND ON REEFS AND THROUGHOUT THE OCEANS.

Because of its highly successful propagation program, the aquarium has been able to fully stock its exhibits with live coral, and the result is stunning. "With living corals, the exhibits always look great," says Delbeek. "They provide a vibrant and natural environment, which causes the fish to behave in more interesting ways. A lot of aquarium hobbyists that come here from the mainland gaze in awe at the sheer color and beauty of our exhibits."

Many other aquariums now seek to stock their exhibits with live coral. So, too, do an increasing number of individual collectors. Much of the coral that supplies this growing market is gathered on natural reefs, causing damage to sensitive environmental systems already under severe pressure.

"By supplying corals to public institutions, we can help alleviate some of the collection pressure," says Delbeek.

Coral gathering is only one of several factors contributing to a decline in the size and health of reefs throughout the world. Mechanical dredging and silting are wreaking havoc with ancient reefs along some coasts, while an increase in water temperature caused by global warming may be damaging reefs everywhere. Since coral reefs are not just beautiful but also vitally important biologically, geologically, and economically, their loss would be calamitous for the planet and all who live on it.

The giant reefs of the Hawaiian Islands are also threatened. Hawaii is a natural home for coral, and tremendous quantities of it grow here. Oddly enough, the diversity of corals found on Hawaiian reefs is relatively low. While there are a few species found only in Hawaiian waters, many others do not grow here at all.

CHARLES DELBEEK CHECKS ON CONDITIONS IN A CORAL FARM PROPAGATION TANK.

"There's a lot of coral here," says Delbeek. "But what you tend to see are very specific stands, meaning only one or two species cover a wide area of reef."

It may be that Hawaiian coral stands were once more diverse. If that is true, no one is sure why reef diversity has declined. However, if species diversity is decreasing, there may be a way to reverse the trend.

"One of our current projects is what we call the Hawaiian Ark Tank," says Delbeek. "Basically, that's a holding tank for rare Hawaiian corals. Our long-term goal is to propagate these corals and return them to local Hawaiian reefs."

THIS DEEPWATER ANTHIAS DELIVERS A SILENT MESSAGE: ITS WORLD IS ALSO OUR WORLD.

Theoretically, the same might be done for reef systems around the world, even ones that have been severely damaged. By taking branches from aquarium propagation tanks or from large colonies in the wild and replanting them, it may be possible eventually to grow vast new colonies and bring new life to our planet's dying reefs.

Native Hawaiians find the aquarium's conservation message and propagation efforts appealing, for they have always felt close to the ocean. It is a kinship deeply rooted in their culture and their religion. Dean Spencer thinks that should be true for us all.

"That's what I want to say to every visitor who comes to Hawaii," says Spencer. "It's terribly important that we take care of what we have, because twenty years from now it may not be there for our children to see and enjoy. As they say in Hawaiian, 'Take care of the sea, for it brings you life.'"

Appendix
Public Aquariums in the United States

Each of the aquariums listed below features its own varied and colorful menagerie of marine life, as well as changing exhibits and events you won't want to miss. Many offer special opportunities for children, including camps, sleepovers, and other stimulating educational experiences. Some are available to host business meetings, reunions, birthday parties, and even weddings. Nearly all maintain membership and volunteer programs entitling participants to enjoy their facilities to the fullest. Aquarium Web sites detail featured exhibits, programs, and offerings. Since many aquariums have seasonal hours, it is wise to check the Web site or call ahead when planning a visit.

Alaska

Alaska SeaLife Center
Milepost 0 Seward Highway
301 Railway Avenue
P.O. Box 1329
Seward, AK 99664
(800) 224-2525
alaskasealife.org

Open daily year-round

The Alaska SeaLife Center combines research with wildlife rescue and public education in a cold-water marine science facility. Ironically, the center owes its existence in part to one of history's greatest ecological disasters—the grounding of the oil tanker *Exxon Valdez* on March 24, 1989, and subsequent oil spill that killed huge numbers of animals in Alaska's once-pristine Prince William Sound. Nearly half the facility's $56 million cost was provided by the settlement fund established after the accident.

THIS HARBOR SEAL HELPS SEALIFE CENTER SCIENTISTS WITH THEIR RESEARCH. THE SEAL'S NAME IS QILAK, WHICH MEANS CLOUD.

The center, which opened in spring 1998, is dedicated to maintaining the integrity of Alaska's marine ecosystem through research, rehabilitation, and public education. The center maintains three on-site 1,500-square-foot laboratories that facilitate research on marine mammals, fish, and invertebrates. Research projects focus on ecological change and seek to identify the causes of the recent alarming declines in worldwide populations of harbor seals, eiders, and Steller's sea lions. The center's medical care and rehabilitation programs for abandoned, injured, or stranded marine mammals are helping maintain healthy populations of these animals in the Gulf of Alaska while providing important information about regional wildlife.

For the general public, the center offers an unrivaled opportunity for close-up views of Steller's sea lions, puffins, Alaskan king crabs, sea stars, giant Pacific octopuses, and rarely seen deep-sea fish. Exhibits allow visitors to observe sea animals in very natural habitats as well as in research settings. The center offers education programs for all ages from preschool to Elderhostel. These are designed to expand the public's awareness of Alaska's marine ecosystem and of the growing threats to its integrity.

THE 156,000-SQUARE-FOOT AQUARIUM OF THE PACIFIC COMPLEX HOUSES MORE THAN 12,000 ANIMALS.

California

Aquarium of the Pacific
100 Aquarium Way
Long Beach, CA 90802
(562) 590–3100
www.aquariumofpacific.org

Open daily except Christmas and the weekend of the Grand Prix of Long Beach, usually held in April

Located in beautiful Rainbow Harbor on Long Beach, the Aquarium of the Pacific is the fifth largest aquarium in the United States. Indeed, with more

VISITORS AT THE ALASKA SEALIFE CENTER WILL SEE SEALS, SEABIRDS, AND A SEEMINGLY ENDLESS VARIETY OF OTHER AQUATIC CREATURES. THE CALIFORNIA SEA LION AT THE RIGHT IS NAMED MILLER, AND HE LIVES AT THE AQUARIUM OF THE PACIFIC.

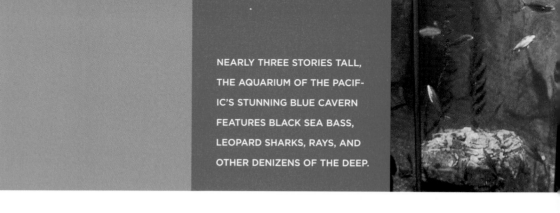

IT'S NOT EVERY DAY YOU GET TO PET A SHARK, BUT YOU CAN AT THE AQUARIUM OF THE PACIFIC.

than 12,000 ocean animals representing more than 550 aquatic species on exhibit and 156,000-plus square feet of floor space in which to display them, this aquarium makes a big impression.

The aquarium is big enough, in fact, to take visitors on a voyage of discovery that spans three distinct regions of the world's greatest ocean—the tropical South Pacific, the chilly North Pacific, and, closer to home, the coastal waters of Southern and Baja California. The complete journey takes some time and requires stops at eighteen major habitats and thirty-one more tightly focused exhibits. Among the highlights here are the 350,000-gallon Tropical Reef Habitat, the three-story-high Blue Cavern, and the popular Harbor Seal and Sea Lion Tunnel.

Despite its size and the ambition of its exhibits, the Aquarium of the Pacific is no Hollywood spectacular. This not-for-profit, public educational facility is thoroughly committed to conservation and, according to its stated mission, "instilling a sense of wonder, respect, and stewardship of the Pacific Ocean and its inhabitants" through education, beautiful displays, and conservation.

Aquarium of the Bay
Embarcadero at Beach Street
Pier 39
San Francisco, CA 94133
(415) 623-5300
www.aquariumofthebay.com

Open daily except Christmas

In 1996 San Francisco got a new and impressive bay window with the opening of the Aquarium of the Bay on the famed Embarcadero. As its name suggests, the aquarium was intended to celebrate the wildlife of San Francisco Bay—one of the world's liveliest and most sensitive ecosystems—and that is exactly what it does. By educating its visitors, the aquarium hopes to inspire a will to preserve this extraordinary marine resource. But entertainment is also part of the mix, and there is plenty of that to enjoy.

A moving walkway conveys visitors through a pair of 300-foot-long clear-walled tunnels where they can get almost within touching distance of the wildlife typical of both the bay and the deep water beyond the Golden Gate. Surrounded by 700,000 gallons of filtered bay water, the tunnels provide an insider's perspective on the habitats and daily lives of bat rays, rare angel sharks, and countless other species. There are more than 23,000 bay and ocean creatures on display here, and naturalists are always at hand to answer questions. Not just a showplace, the aquarium also conducts research and promotes species conservation through education.

THIS TROPICAL REEF EXHIBIT AT THE BIRCH AQUARIUM LOOKS LIKE A PAINTING.

Birch Aquarium at Scripps
University of California, San Diego
9500 Gilman Drive, Department 0207
La Jolla, CA 92093
(858) 534-4086
aquarium.ucsd.edu

Open daily year-round

Set against a breathtaking view of the Pacific, the Birch Aquarium is home to more than 350 species of marine life found throughout a wide swath of ocean, from the icy waters of the Northwest to the warm tropical reefs of the Pacific Ocean's equatorial regions. Operated as part of the famed Scripps Institution of Oceanography, the Birch Aquarium provides marine science education, interprets research conducted at Scripps, and promotes ocean conservation. Its forty-six exhibits range from a 70,000-gallon tank housing a forest of kelp down to small nursery tanks not much larger than a home aquarium. Outside the main building, man-made tide pools allow visitors

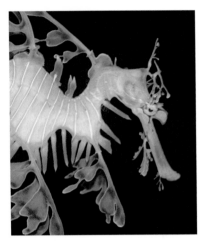

THE BIRCH AQUARIUM OFFERS WORLD-CLASS DISPLAYS OF SEAHORSES AND RELATED SPECIES SUCH AS LEAFY SEA DRAGONS, WHICH ARE WELL EQUIPPED FOR HIDING IN UNDERWATER FOLIAGE.

to see and learn about coastal environments that exist right on San Diego's doorstep.

Visitors can take a simulated submersible ride, track up-to-the-minute earthquake and tsunami data, or visit the "Ocean Supermarket" to scan grocery items and learn where in the sea they come from. Classes and programs for all ages provide more in-depth opportunities to learn about and interact with such marine animals as gray whales and sharks.

Seahorses are a specialty of this aquarium. On display are thirteen seahorse species from waters both near and far. Exhibits explore the unique adaptations and biology that cause seahorses to look as they do—like miniature legless horses with coiled tails. Few visitors believe these animals are in any way related to horses, but most have difficulty believing the truth—that they are actually a kind of fish. True to its conservation mission, the aquarium is a leader in the propagation of seahorses and so far has successfully bred ten different species. During the last decade, seahorses bred at the Birch Aquarium have been

KIDS ALWAYS LOVE THE SHARKS AT THE BIRCH AQUARIUM AT SCRIPPS.

OUTDOOR EXHIBITS PROVIDE A VIEW OF THE PACIFIC, THE NATIVE HABITAT OF MANY BIRCH AQUARIUM ANIMALS.

Monterey Bay Aquarium
886 Cannery Row
Monterey, CA 93940
(831) 648-4800
www.mbayaq.org

Open daily except Christmas

Founded during the 1980s with money provided by the Packard Foundation, the Monterey Bay Aquarium is a "new generation" facility focusing on local species and emphasizing natural habitat displays. Most exhibits are supplied with water pumped directly from the relatively unpolluted bay. During the day the water is filtered so that visitors can get a better look at the animals on display. At night, however, unfiltered water brings with it large quantities of algae and microorganisms that nourish the exhibits and make them almost identical to the habitats found in the bay.

shipped to more than fifty zoos and aquariums, thus reducing the demand for collecting them from the wild.

Cabrillo Marine Aquarium
3720 Stephen White Drive
San Pedro, CA 90731
(310) 548-7562
www.cabrilloaq.org

Open daily year-round; closed Monday

A facility of the City of the Los Angeles Department of Recreation and Parks, the Cabrillo Marine Aquarium is located near Cabrillo Beach in San Pedro between Point Fermin and the Port of Los Angeles. An educational, recreational, and research facility devoted to the marine life of Southern California, the aquarium encourages active public participation in its conserva-

tion efforts. Exhibits focus on a wide variety of habitats, including kelp forest, rocky shore, mudflats, Channel Islands, sandy beach, and open ocean. Of particular interest is an exhibit on oil rigs and their impact on marine life.

Visitors can add to the benefits of a day at the aquarium by walking to nearby Point Fermin Marine Life Refuge, with its tide pools, salt marshes, beaches, and other coastal habitats. The combination of indoor exhibits and outdoor experiences make this an excellent area for teaching or learning about marine biology, conservation, and a host of other topics. The aquarium offers a library and educational programs for teachers, students, and the general public.

A BIG TUNA IS BROUGHT TO THE MONTEREY BAY AQUARIUM ON A STRETCHER.

Among the highlights here is the Kelp Forest exhibit. This 335,000-gallon tank and swaying forest of giant kelp that grows in it provide shelter for a host of fish and other marine animals. The aquarium has built on the success of its Kelp Forest and other true-to-nature exhibits, establishing one of the largest and finest jellyfish displays in the world. The mesmerizing jellyfish exhibits convey the impression that these diaphanous creatures are living works of art, and it is hard to see them without emotion.

Some of the jellyfish are located in the aquarium's Outer Bay wing, which plunges visitors into the murky depths of the bay—dropping down into a canyon more than 2 miles beneath the surface, it is very deep indeed—by way of a million-gallon tank fitted with an enormous acrylic window. Inside the tank, schools of large tuna, sharks, turtles, and other open-ocean creatures remain constantly in motion.

The Monterey Bay Aquarium is second to none in the promotion of conservation. Much work is being done

MONTEREY BAY AQUARIUM STAFFERS WORK THE BAY IN SEARCH OF LOCAL SPECIES TO FILL DISPLAY TANKS.

here to preserve native species. A project of special interest to both scientists and the public is a sea otter rescue and rehabilitation program. These endangered coastal mammals have become a favored icon of the aquarium.

SeaWorld San Diego
500 SeaWorld Drive
San Diego, CA 92109
(619) 222-6363
www.4adventure.com/seaworld/ca

Open daily year-round

One of several similar attractions owned and operated by the Anheuser-Busch Company and located in major tourist destinations across the country, SeaWorld San Diego is part theme park, part resort, and part aquarium. This venue offers 189 acres of rides, entertainments, physical challenges, exhibits, and performing animal shows. Certainly the most famous of the animals on display here is Shamu, one of several killer whales, or orcas, in residence. The orcas are stars of SeaWorld's spectacular performances in part because they can swim at speeds of up to 30 miles per hour and leap high in the air. Extremely intelligent, they are also easy to train. SeaWorld offers adventure camps for children and educational programs on subjects such as polar bears, penguins, sharks, reefs, tide pools, manatees, and wildlife rescue.

RAYS PUT ON A WATERY BALLET AT THE MONTEREY BAY AQUARIUM.

Connecticut

The Maritime Aquarium at Norwalk
10 North Water Street
Norwalk, CT 06854
(203) 852-0700
www.maritimeaquarium.org

**Open daily except Thanksgiving
and Christmas**

One of only a few aquariums in the country devoted to one body of water, the Marine Aquarium of Norwalk explores both the sea life and maritime culture of Long Island Sound. More than 1,000 animals are on display, and although all are indigenous to the sound, they represent a surprising variety of species. Exhibits portray a range of habitats, from shallow tidal zones alive with oysters, seahorses, and small fish to the open ocean with its sharks, rays, and big commercial fishes. Harbor seals, jellyfish, loggerhead sea turtles, and many other species are also on display. The Ocean Playspace on the second floor of the aquarium

THE WORD "SCHOOL" TAKES ON A WHOLE NEW MEANING AT THE MARITIME AQUARIUM.

provides a protected area for young children while introducing them to sea life and promoting motor skills, imagination, interactive play, coordination, balance, and sensory awareness.

MARINE LIFE CRUISES (LEFT) OFFER PARTICIPANTS A CHANCE TO MEET SHARKS AND OTHER SEA CREATURES IN THEIR HOME ENVIRONMENT, BUT PLENTY OF SHARKS (CENTER) AND SEALS (RIGHT) ARE ON DISPLAY AT THE MARITIME AQUARIUM AT NORWALK.

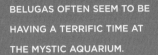
BELUGAS OFTEN SEEM TO BE
HAVING A TERRIFIC TIME AT
THE MYSTIC AQUARIUM.

THIS HARBOR SEAL AT THE MARITIME
AQUARIUM IS KNOWN TO HER
FRIENDS AS POLLY.

Mystic Aquarium
55 Coogan Boulevard
Mystic, CT 06355
(860) 572–5955
store.mysticaquarium.org

**Open daily except Thanksgiving
and Christmas**

Most people in the United States
have heard of Mystic Seaport, a
museum devoted to the maritime
culture and history of New England,
but the Mystic Aquarium is less well
known. Even so, it has much to offer
in the way of well-designed exhibits
and sea creatures such as sharks,
beluga whales, rays, seals, sea lions,
exotic frogs, and dapper penguins.
Mystic Aquarium is active in the rescue and rehabilitation of stranded
and injured whales, seals, and penguins.

SEA ANEMONES AND COLD-WATER
PENGUINS ARE ALL PART OF THE
SHOW AT CONNECTICUT'S MYSTIC
AQUARIUM.

WITH THEIR FLEXIBLE NECKS AND READY SMILES, MYSTIC AQUARIUM'S BELUGAS
ARE VERY EXPRESSIVE.

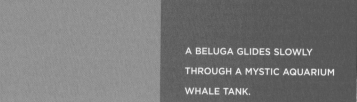

CARELESS HUMAN POWERBOAT PILOTS ARE THE MANATEE'S WORST ENEMY, BUT
THESE MOTE MARINE AQUARIUM VISITORS ARE DEFINITELY FRIENDS.

Florida

The Florida Aquarium
701 Channelside Drive
Tampa. FL 33602
(813) 273-4000
www.flaquarium.net

**Open daily except Thanksgiving
and Christmas**

This downtown Tampa aquarium features animals and plants from Tampa Bay, Florida, and beyond. Established in 1995 the facility has attracted millions of visitors and has brought an estimated $60 million per year into the area economy.

A signature of the aquarium is its unusual dome. Rooftop tours provide a close inspection of this architectural wonder while allowing visitors to peer down into the aquarium's largest tanks. Most prominent of these is the 500,000-gallon Coral Reef tank, which supports 1,600 animals from sixty separate species, all of them native to Florida. A special aquarium scuba program allows visitors to actually dive into the reef tank and explore its wonders from the inside. They can also dive into the 93,000-gallon shark tank and have an adventure they'll be talking about for years.

Visitors can get behind the aquarium scenes in other ways as well. For instance, they can visit the kitchens where chefs prepare food for 10,000 animals, including many sea creatures with very special diets. Freezers in the kitchen are stuffed with veggie gel, gator chow, and lots of other goodies for aquarium residents. Then of course there is plenty of fresh seafood not much different in kind or quality than what one might be served in a fine Tampa restaurant.

Aquarium explorations extend well beyond the building itself in the form of Ecotours of Tampa Bay. These tours aboard a sleek, 64-foot catamaran boost the Florida Aquarium's efforts to promote "ocean stewardship" by pointing out the impact of pollution and rampant development along the shores of the bay.

The bay has other problems as well—it has been invaded by a number of troublesome nonnative species, such as the walking catfish and giant marine toad. Populations of these and other exotic flora and fauna brought to the area by ships or in other ways have exploded, driving many beneficial local species out of the area. Aquarium visitors can learn about these invaders and what is being done to stop them.

In addition to its exhibits and education programs, the aquarium is active in sea turtle rehabilitation, coral propagation, seahorse conservation, breeding river otters, and a regional watch placed on the dwindling population of manatees.

Mote Marine Aquarium
1600 Ken Thompson Parkway
Sarasota, FL 34236
(941) 388-4441
www.mote.org

Open daily year-round

Part of the well-known Mote Marine Laboratory, this aquarium highlights Florida's fascinating marine life through a combination of entertainment and education. It also throws a spotlight on the valuable research being done at the laboratory. Sharks are a prominent attraction here, and a unique Shark Sensory Theater enables visitors to experience the ocean environment in much the way

these powerful hunters do—through their senses. Other sensory experiences include a hands-on touch tank, where children and adults can pet rays or nudge horseshoe crabs, and an Immersion Cinema, where audiences can participate in shows about dolphins, the marine food web, and predation.

Manatees are even rarer in captivity than they are in the wild, but this aquarium has a pair on display. Their names are Hugh and Buffet, and they are very hungry creatures. In a day's time they're likely to consume more than eighty heads of lettuce along with a smorgasbord of apples, beets, carrots, kale, monkey biscuits, and vitamins. No wonder their combined weight of several thousand pounds is more than that of an average automobile.

A key attraction of the facility is its working laboratories, where visitors can catch a glimpse of marine science in the making as scientists study red tide, cancer resistance in sharks, and the human impact on fragile marine environments. Special eco-boat tours allow visitors to explore the coastal environment with trained staff.

SeaWorld

7007 SeaWorld Drive
Orlando, FL 32821
(407) 351-3600
www.4adventure.com/seaworld/fla

Open daily year-round

Located about ten minutes south of Orlando, SeaWorld brings its own marine adventure theme along with

SEA TURTLES ARE ENDANGERED, AND MOTE MARINE AQUARIUM RESEARCHERS ARE ANXIOUS TO FIND OUT WHAT CAN BE DONE TO SAVE THEM.

ALTHOUGH NOT NECESSARILY UNHAPPY, BLUEFIN TREVALLY TUNA WEAR A NATURALLY GRIM EXPRESSION AT WAIKIKI AQUARIUM.

200 acres of rides, shows, and animal exhibits to this land of mega-parks and resorts. More than eighty million visitors have toured SeaWorld and been entertained by its killer whales, dolphins, stingrays, and sea lions. One of several SeaWorld parks scattered around the country, this one is much like the others, only larger, and it is able to host sizable conventions. Educational programs and adventure camps are available for children.

Walt Disney World Resort
Living Seas Pavilion
Lake Buena Vista, FL 32830
(407) 560-7688
http://disneyworld.disney.go.com

Open daily year-round

Although the Living Seas Pavilion is only one of many attractions at the Walt Disney World Resort, it is nonetheless impressive. In fact, it houses the world's largest saltwater aquarium tank. More than 200 feet in diameter and 27 feet deep, the tank holds an astounding 5.7 million gallons of seawater, about as much as the combined capacity of all the display tanks in a very large public aquarium. On exhibit either in the big tank or in smaller tanks are many of the sea creatures you might expect to find in such a venue—dolphins, sharks, and thousands of tropical fish. One species you might not expect to see is the endangered manatee, but there are several in residence—all rescued, perhaps after unhappy encounters with power-boats and propellers. Visitors can watch marine science in the making at the pavilion's Sea Base Alpha, a working undersea research facility. Certified scuba divers can don a wetsuit and take a guided tour inside the big tank.

Hawaii

Maui Ocean Center
192 Ma'alaea Road
Wailuku, HI 96793
(808) 270-7000
www.mauioceancenter.com

Open daily year-round

Located on Ma'alaea Harbor, the Maui Ocean Center is a marine park dedicated to fostering understanding, wonder, and respect for Hawaii's marine culture. All the animals on exhibit were gathered from the fertile waters and reefs off the Hawaiian Islands, and many are endemic, meaning they are found only in Hawaiian waters. Drawing on a quarter century of diving, research, and study, the center displays these animals in highly realistic native habitats so that visitors can gain a deeper understanding of Hawaii's unique

A DIVER SHOWS OFF AN EAGLE RAY AT THE MAUI OCEAN CENTER.

MAUI OCEAN CENTER'S REALISTIC OUTDOOR EXHIBITS ARE BETTER FOR BOTH ANIMALS AND VISITORS.

A CLOWNFISH PEEKS FROM A PROTECTIVE THICKET OF SEA ANEMONE IN THIS WAIKIKI AQUARIUM DISPLAY.

aquatic environment. Interactive displays, outdoor touch pools, and an acrylic tunnel through the 750,000-gallon Open Ocean exhibit allow visitors to experience the islands' marine life up close. Throughout the day, naturalists are on hand at the aquarium's well-designed Living Reef, Turtle Lagoon, Hammerhead Harbor, Discovery Pool, and Open Ocean exhibits to share insights on life beneath the waves.

The center emphasizes community education and seeks to promote a lifelong bond between visitors and the ocean and deeper appreciation of its wonders. Aquarium educational efforts include an annual Coral Spawning event, which provides a highly unusual glimpse at the "sex lives" of animals that many people imagine are merely hunks of rock. Monthly Sea Talks feature noted marine specialists or cultural representatives. Regular educational tours and special events are offered to Hawaiian school children.

Sea Life Park
41-202 Kalanianaole Highway
Suite 7
Waimanolo, HI 96795
(808) 259-7933
www.sealifeparkhawaii.com

Open daily year-round

Fifteen miles from Waikiki, on Oahu's Makapuu Point, Sea Life Park offers rides and other tourist attractions as well as up-to-date marine life exhibits that emphasize education and conservation. A special park highlight is its 300,000-gallon Hawaiian Reef tank, which features more than 2,000 animals, including sharks, rays, and a wide variety of multicolored tropical fish. The aquarium's Sea Trek experience allows vis-

TOUCH TANKS ADD ANOTHER SENSORY DIMENSION TO THE AQUARIUM EXPERIENCE AT THE MAUI OCEAN CENTER.

itors to actually enter the tank to get the closest possible view of its inhabitants.

Other exhibits such as the Stingray Lagoon, Sea Turtle Lagoon, and Sea Bird Sanctuary carry visitors beyond the reef into other island habitats. An Ocean Theater treats visitors to dolphins performing in a large wrap-around glass tank. Special park programs allow some visitors to personally interact with the dolphins. A portion of the park admission price goes toward marine animal rescue and rehabilitation programs.

Waikiki Aquarium
2777 Kalakaua Avenue
Honolulu, HI 96815
(808) 923-9741
waquarium.mic.hawaii.edu

Open daily year-round

Located in beautiful Queen Kapiolani Park, on the southern shoreline of the island of Oahu and next to a living reef just offshore, the Waikiki Aquarium is the third oldest public aquarium in the United States. Founded in 1904 and affiliated with the University of Hawaii, the aquarium encompasses exhibits, educational opportunities, and research programs focused on the aquatic life of Hawaii and the tropical Pacific. Visitors can see more than 2,500 animals representing at least 420 species, including many endangered and threatened animals.

Visitors can enjoy close-up views of reef sharks, rare Hawaiian monk seals, graceful sea jellies, and schools of colorful reef fish, but the highlight of this aquarium is clearly its coral. The Waikiki Aquarium was among the first to propagate live

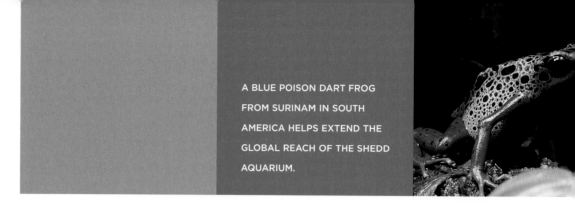

corals and include them in its exhibits. The aquarium also specializes in natural lighting. During daylight hours, most of its exhibits are lit only by the sun, and the effect of this on the displays is stunning.

Deeply committed to conservation, the Waikiki Aquarium is a leader in marine research related to threatened species such as the chambered nautilus and monk seal. The aquarium keeps two rare monk seals on display, which serve as ambassadors for their endangered wild relatives.

A BRIGHTLY COLORED BAT STAR CLINGS TO A ROCK AT THE SHEDD.

Illinois

John G. Shedd Aquarium
1200 South Lake Shore Drive
Chicago, IL 60605
(312) 939-2438
www.sheddaquarium.org

Open daily except Christmas

Although located much nearer the continental heartland than the ocean, the Shedd ranks among the world's foremost aquariums. The Shedd's publicity promotes itself as the "world's aquarium," and that's not just hype. Its focus is truly global, and its exhibits sample waters as far away as the atolls of the South Pacific or as close by as Lake Michigan.

Named for the Chicago businessman who provided much of its early funding, the Shedd opened in 1929, a time when zoos and aquariums displayed their animals in relatively small, discrete exhibits as though they were oddities on a collector's shelf. The early Shedd followed this

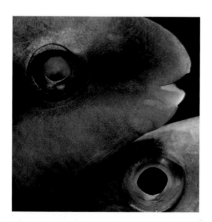
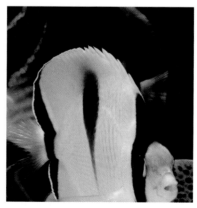
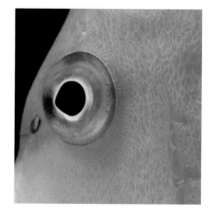

IT'S HARD TO SAY WHAT THEIR EYES PERCEIVE, BUT AQUATIC ANIMALS ARE MORE CLOSELY RELATED TO ONE ANOTHER AND TO US THAN WE MAY THINK.

UNDERWATER TUNNELS SUR-
ROUND VISITORS WITH SEA LIFE
AT THE NEWPORT AQUARIUM.

VISITORS CAN SEE TROPICAL FISH IN
THEIR NATURAL HABITAT AT THE
SHEDD.

that give visitors the feeling they are actually swimming among the sharks. But the exhibit's most striking characteristic is the meticulous detail with which it re-creates the reef environment.

Kentucky

Newport Aquarium
One Aquarium Way
Newport, KY 41071
(859) 261-7444
www.newportaquarium.com

Open daily year-round

Located across the Ohio River from Cincinnati, the Newport Aquarium is one of the nation's most impressive newer aquariums. Its million gallons of fresh and salt waters are home to more than 600 aquatic species and

more than 7,000 animals. Some 380,000 gallons of seawater are devoted to a massive shark tank, probably the facility's most popular exhibit.

Completed in 1999, the Newport Aquarium takes advantage of recent concepts and technologies with, for instance, at least 200 feet of see-through underwater tunnels. To increase the feeling of being immersed in water, the acrylic tunnels were constructed without joints, so there are no distracting metal braces. Walk-around exhibits allow visitors to examine them from all sides.

In contrast to the advanced technology of the exhibits, aquarium walls are covered with seventeen huge hand-painted murals depicting a Louisiana bayou, a coral reef, an arctic land/seascape complete with polar

display scheme, and it can still be seen in older parts of the aquarium. In recent decades, however, the Shedd has embraced the habitat-oriented philosophy of newer aquariums that emphasize environment.

A pair of extensive additions have more than doubled the size of the original structure. The Oceanarium features a three-million-gallon tank, which is home to rare beluga whales, white-sided dolphins, seals, and sea otters. The daily performances of whales and dolphins at the Oceanarium are the aquarium's most popular attraction.

The second addition, built partly underground, houses the Wild Reef exhibit. Depicting the life-rich environment of a Philippine reef, the exhibit includes extra-modern features, such as immersion tunnels

NEWPORT AQUARIUM'S MENACING SHARKS AND OTHER LARGE PREDATORS ARE
ALWAYS POPULAR WITH VISITORS.

A DIVER SPEAKS TO VISITORS WHO ENJOY A CARIBBEAN REEF EXHIBIT FROM A BELOW-SURFACE TUNNEL IN THE AUDUBON AQUARIUM OF THE AMERICAS.

bears, and other aquatic scenes. Created by a local artist, the murals provide an old-fashioned, even homey touch.

The aquarium exhibits are by no means down home, however. They take visitors to every ocean and continent on the planet. In addition to the shark tank, there is a walk-through giant kelp forest, a rain forest exhibit depicting the Amazon in flood, a bayou exhibit complete with alligators, a South Pacific exhibit featuring giant octopuses, a coral reef, and a jellyfish gallery.

Louisiana

Audubon Aquarium of the Americas
Canal Street at the River
1 Canal Street
New Orleans, LA 70130
(800) 774-7394
www.auduboninstitute.org

Open daily year-round

Fresh water meets seawater at the Audubon Aquarium of the Americas, located on the banks of the Mississippi River in the French Quarter of New Orleans. The aquarium spans the underwater world of the Caribbean Sea, the mysterious Amazon rain forest, and the waters that gave birth to New Orleans itself: the Mississippi River and the Gulf of Mexico. The most distinct feature of this aquarium is its Mississippi River gallery, where catfish, paddlefish, and alligators remind us that our planet's vast aquatic realm is not limited to whales, sharks, dolphins, and coral reefs. The Mississippi Delta swamps have been described as a much smaller but nonetheless extraordinary version of the Amazon

basin, and the Audubon Aquarium allows visitors to make this comparison for themselves. Its Amazon Gallery celebrates the world's largest freshwater drainage system, an environmentally threatened area roughly the size of the United States.

The aquarium's Caribbean and Gulf of Mexico displays include sharks, sea turtles, rays, and thousands of multicolored fish. One would expect conservation to be an important emphasis in an aquarium that carries the name of John James Audubon, the early-nineteenth-century naturalist whose highly artistic renderings are all that remain of some of America's extinct bird species. The aquarium sponsors sea turtle and marine mammal rescue programs and many other conservation initiatives. Education is an important focus as well, and the aquarium offers a number of school outreach programs and adventure camps for children.

Maine

Gulf of Maine Research Institute
350 Commercial Street
P.O. Box 7549
Portland, ME 04112
(207) 772-2321
http://octopus.gma.org

Formerly known as the Gulf of Maine Aquarium, this facility has reinvented itself as well as changed its name. The idea is to create a full-fledged scientific and research organization, and the new approach seems to be working. The institute has attracted local, regional, and national interest to its research initiatives focused on a wide range of topics such as glob-

al warming, commercial fisheries, and, of course, life in the Gulf of Maine. The facility's public programs emphasize education.

Maryland

Calvert Marine Museum
14150 Solomons Island Road (State Route 2)
P.O. Box 97
Solomons, MD 20688
(410) 326-2042
www.calvertmarinemuseum.com

Open daily year-round

The Calvert Marine Museum treats its patrons to a range of experiences and displays, all related to the natural history and culture of the southern Maryland shore. Among its exhibits, which are not limited to marine life, are fifteen tanks, ranging in size up to 3,500 gallons. These contain aquatic plants and animals from habitats located between the salty waters of Chesapeake Bay and the fresh water of the upper Patuxent River. An exhibit of rays and skates carries the rather delightful name Secrets of the Mermaid's Purse. The museum complex includes wood carvings, models, a collection of historic boats, and the old Drum Point Lighthouse.

National Aquarium in Baltimore
501 East Pratt Street, Pier 3
Baltimore, MD 21202
(410) 576-3822
www.aqua.org

Open daily except Thanksgiving and Christmas

Located in Baltimore's popular Inner Harbor shopping, dining, and museum district, the National Aquarium is

WRAPAROUND TANKS PUT VISITORS AT THE CENTER OF THE ACTION AT THE NATIONAL AQUARIUM IN BALTIMORE.

Maryland's leading tourist attraction—and it is not hard to see why. A distinctly modern facility with an enormous tank much like the one at the New England Aquarium in Boston, it is far more than a place to see strange-looking sea creatures. This aquarium treats visitors to an *experience* much more akin to a drama or documentary than a walk through a museum. Visitors move upward through several levels, each with its own tanks and animals and each devoted to a different aspect of the sea-life saga.

As visitors enter the aquarium and ascend the levels, they encounter a series of stunning exhibit galleries. Among these are Wings in the Water (featuring sharks and rays), Mountains to the Sea (fresh water streams, ponds, tidal marshes, crabs, terrapin, small fish, and invertebrates),

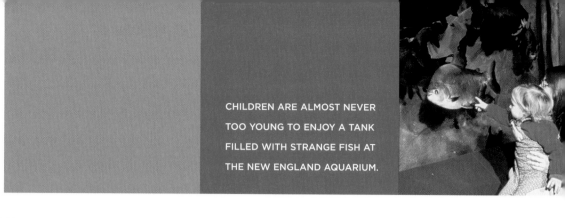

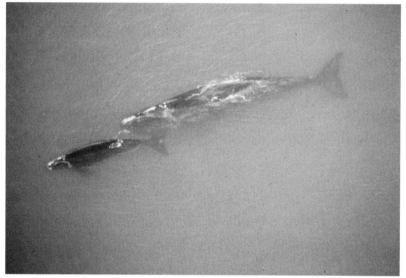

NEW ENGLAND AQUARIUM RESEARCHERS KEEP CLOSE TABS ON ENDANGERED RIGHT WHALES SUCH AS THIS MOTHER AND CALF IN THE BAY OF FUNDY.

Surviving through Adaptation (electric eels, sea urchins, octopuses, and sturgeon), Puffins (North Atlantic seabirds), Amazon River Forest (river turtles, caimans, and marmosets), Atlantic Coral Reef (vividly colored tropical fish), Open Ocean (big tiger and nurse sharks), and several other impressive exhibit areas. A bridge links the main lobby to the Marine Mammal Pavilion, with its wildly popular dolphins. The aquarium houses more than 560 species and 10,500 individual animals.

The aquarium hosts special tours and programs designed to inspire visitors to become involved in the marine world around them. These provide behind-the-scenes tours of the aquarium wildlife rescue facility, hospital pools for sick or injured animals, and the kitchens where tons of food are prepared daily for the thousands of sea creatures that inhabit the exhibits. A wide variety of education programs and conservation-related events also are offered.

Massachusetts

New England Aquarium
Central Wharf
Boston, MA 02110
(617) 973-5200
www.neaq.org

Open daily year-round

Just a short walk from Faneuil Hall, Quincy Market, and other popular Boston tourist destinations, the New England Aquarium is the focal attraction of the city's old harbor waterfront district. Described by many as the "first truly modern aquarium," the structure was designed by Peter Chermayeff, a young, innovative architect. His concept called for a large central tank with an ascending series of exhibit galleries wrapped around it, providing visitors with a documentary-like experience. (Indeed, Chermayeff had dabbled in film documentaries before he took the assignment.)

The New England Aquarium is home to thousands of sea creatures representing hundreds of species. A favorite of many visitors, and of aquarium staff as well, Myrtle is a green sea turtle that lives in and dominates the big central exhibit known as the Giant Ocean Tank. Some 40 feet in diameter and 21 feet deep, the big tank holds about 200,000 gallons of water and is home to 700 animals representing 130 species. Visitors can gaze into the tank from many different angles through fifty-two large windows. The shimmering light escaping through the windows makes the entire aquarium feel as though it is underwater.

The aquarium sponsors several programs aimed at saving ocean species, most notably Kemp's Ridley turtles and right whales. Aquarium scientists take part in extensive field research, nearly all of it related to conservation. The aquarium's rescue-and-release programs have saved hundreds if not thousands of hapless animals, many of them endangered turtles. To promote a more ocean-friendly approach to fishing, the aquarium works with consumers as well as seafood distributors and retailers through a program called EcoSound. Camps and education programs run by aquarium staff strive for an even loftier goal, however—that of inspiring true environmental stewardship through an appreciation of the oceans and their importance to our own lives.

A GREEN MORAY EEL IN THE GLOVER'S REEF EXHIBIT AT THE NEW YORK AQUARIUM.

New Jersey

Adventure Aquarium (New Jersey State Aquarium)
1 Riverside Drive
Camden, NJ 08103
(856) 365-3300
www.adventureaquarium.com

Open daily except Thanksgiving, Christmas, and New Year's Day

Situated on Camden's waterfront opposite historic Penn's Landing in Philadelphia, the New Jersey State Aquarium seeks to promote public appreciation of the state's wide-spread and, in many cases, threatened aquatic habitats and a will to protect them. The aquarium combines an extensive hands-on education program for students from preschool through high school with breathtaking displays. The exhibits contain thousands of marine and freshwater creatures representing more than 500 species. The Ocean Base Atlantic Tank, one of the more than eighty exhibits at the aquarium, holds 760,000 gallons of seawater. Divers are often on hand in the Open Ocean Tank to answer visitors' questions via underwater microphones.

The aquarium provides an impressive range of experiences, including a tropical mangrove lagoon, a Caribbean beach, a coral-encrusted shipwreck, and a tank that makes it possible to actually touch sharks and rays. A special exhibit highlights the history and ecology of the Delaware River, Delaware Bay, and the New Jersey Pine Barrens. The aquarium offers a full schedule of activities every day, including performances by divers, seals, sharks, and even snakes. For children there are also sea life–related games, puzzles, and educational programs.

New York

New York Aquarium
Surf Avenue and West Eighth Street
Brooklyn, NY 11224
(718) 265-FISH (3474)
www.nyaquarium.com

Open daily year-round

Where else would the New York Aquarium be but on Coney Island, where the big city meets the sea? The aquarium has been a Coney Island attraction for more than half a century, but it was once located elsewhere—Manhattan, in fact. The oldest continuously operated aquarium in the United States, the New York Aquarium first opened its doors to the public in 1896. At that time it was located in Battery Park, not far from the Staten Island Ferry landing.

A NEW YORK AQUARIUM TRAINER GETS A WET SMOOCH FROM A CALIFORNIA SEA LION.

BERNIE THE HARBOR SEAL APPEARS TO BE CONTEMPLATING A NAP AT THE NEW YORK AQUARIUM.

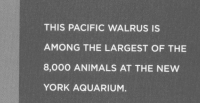

KIDS ENJOY A BENEATH-THE-SURFACE LOOK AT A WHALE IN BELUGA BAY IN THE
NEW YORK AQUARIUM.

The aquarium's existing Conservation Hall was erected on Coney Island in 1957, and it still serves as the first stop for visitors when they arrive at the fourteen-acre facility. Most take a while to get oriented, for this is a large aquarium. With displays featuring 630 species and more than 8,000 animals, the aquarium offers numerous fascinating sights and activities, nearly all of them highly educational. A science-based conservation organization with experts studying wildlife in the field worldwide, the aquarium takes pride in the expertise and educational commitment of its staff. Their goal is to provide sound information to the public and to engender awareness of both the importance of our oceans and the need to protect them.

Like New Yorkers themselves, the animals here come from near and afar—habitats as distant as the South African coast, a third of the way around the globe, or as close by as the Hudson River. As is the case at many other aquariums, the marine mammals here are a big hit with the public. There are several resident walruses, including the exceptionally popular Ayveg, a large male brought here from the Bering Sea in 1994. Ayveg weighed only about 150 pounds when he was abandoned by his mother, rescued, and relocated to New York, but he has put on a little weight since then—about 1,100 pounds. Another aquarium favorite is Willie the Sea Otter. Willie is from California, where he was rescued and raised by the staff of the Monterey Bay Aquarium. Marine

mammals are not the only aquarium creatures given names. Bertha is a resident tiger shark. Nearly thirty years old, she has an impressive set of teeth—about 3,000 of them in all.

North Carolina

North Carolina Aquarium at Fort Fisher
900 Loggerhead Road
Kure Beach, NC 28449
(910) 458-8257
www.ncaquariums.com

Open daily except Thanksgiving, Christmas, and New Year's Day

Located beyond Kure Beach, south of Wilmington, this aquarium is one of several operated by the North Carolina Department of Environment

HOW FAR IN CAN SHE GO? A CHILD
TESTS A BUBBLE WINDOW IN THE
NORTH CAROLINA AQUARIUM.

THE NORTH CAROLINA AQUARIUM DISPLAYS MARINE LIFE AS WELL AS COMMON FRESHWATER ANIMALS SUCH AS THESE ALLIGATORS.

AT THE NORTH CAROLINA AQUARIUM AT FORT FISHER, THE PRESENCE OF SHARKS IN A TANK FAILS TO DETER DIVERS WHO CONSIDER MOST AQUARIUM ANIMALS THEIR FRIENDS.

and Natural Resources. The Fort Fisher Aquarium takes visitors on a journey from the Cape Fear River swamps and saltwater marshes to the reefs and shoals that lie off the North Carolina barrier islands. The aquarium's feature exhibit is a two-story, multilevel tank containing sharks, groupers, loggerhead turtles, barracudas, and many other sea animals. Volunteers are recruited for a number of worthy conservation projects, such as rescue and rehabilitation of sea turtles or cleaning up beaches and wetlands.

North Carolina Aquarium on Roanoke Island
Off Airport Road
P.O. Box 967
Manteo, NC 27954
(252) 473-3493
www.ncaquariums.com

Open daily except Thanksgiving, Christmas, and New Year's Day

Located near the historic town of Manteo on the Outer Banks and overlooking life-rich Croatan Sound, the North Carolina Aquarium on Roanoke Island serves up live demonstrations with alligators, sea

turtles, and snakes. The Graveyard of the Atlantic exhibit features divers who dialogue with visitors outside the tank. The exhibit takes its name from an expression often used by mariners to describe North Carolina's Outer Banks, where thousands of ships have run aground over the centuries and been torn apart by waves. Special events such as a Breakfast with Rays encourage visitors to explore the local marine environment. Facilities include meeting rooms, classrooms, an auditorium, and research space.

ALTHOUGH MANATEES LOOK A BIT LIKE GIANT POTATOES, MANY COLUMBUS AQUARIUM VISITORS FIND THEM ADORABLE.

FEW AQUATIC ANIMALS ARE STRANGER IN APPEARANCE OR MORE DELICATE THAN THE WEEDY SEA DRAGON, A RELATIVE OF THE SEAHORSE, FOUND AT THE COLUMBUS ZOO AND AQUARIUM.

Ohio

Columbus Zoo and Aquarium
9990 Riverside Drive
Powell, Ohio 43065
(614) 645-3400
www.columbuszoo.org

Open daily year-round

Part of a substantial wildlife display complex in Columbus, this aquarium brings the oceans and rivers of the world to Ohio. The range of wildlife, exhibits, and experiences here is considerable. Visitors can watch Humboldt penguins dive from cliffs into their 9,000-gallon pool, visit a tropical coral reef, pet horseshoe crabs and starfish in a touch tank, and study animals as widely separated in habitat and characteristics as jellyfish, flamingos, alligators, and poison arrow frogs.

Perhaps surprisingly, this Midwest aquarium takes a special interest in manatees, which in the wild don't come within a thousand miles of Columbus. Nonetheless, the aquarium keeps a trio of manatees on display and is intimately involved in conservation of this seriously threatened species. Dundee, Gene, a 2,000-pound male, and a juvenile named Turtle were removed from the wild because they could no longer survive on their own. Now they impress Ohio children and adults with their slow-moving, elephantine antics. The aquarium is involved in conservation efforts directed at other species as well, including an internationally recognized breeding program for Lake Victoria cichlids.

Oregon

Oregon Coast Aquarium
2820 Southeast Ferry Slip Road
Newport, OR 97365
(541) 867–3474
www.aquarium.org

Open daily except Christmas

The long, green shoreline of Oregon, sometimes described as the Emerald Coast, is a natural wonder that needs no official celebration. Anyone who has seen it loves it. However, the sea life and water birds that live on or near these spectacular shores may not be as familiar as the scenery. The Oregon Coast Aquarium near Newport is making a creditable effort to correct that and bring both Oregonians and visitors closer to these creatures.

Unlike most other aquariums, this one has placed many of its most popular exhibits outdoors, where they seem part of the environment. Among the outdoor favorites are harbor seals, sea lions, and sea otters. An outdoor aviary features tufted puffins, rhinoceros auklets, pigeon guillemots, common murres, and lots of other wading and diving birds. Inside the aquarium, visitors can explore the habitats of the Pacific Northwest in a 1.32-million-gallon tank connected by a 200-foot underwater tunnel that snakes through the Open Ocean, Halibut Flats, and Orford Reef exhibits. The tunnel provides a nearly 360-degree view of sharks, batfish, wolf eels, and giant octopuses. Like many other aquariums today, the Oregon Coast Aquarium offers educational programs and participates in marine research and conservation programs.

COLUMBUS AQUARIUM CONSERVATION EFFORTS EXTEND TO SEA TURTLES AS WELL AS SEA DRAGONS AND MANATEES.

Pennsylvania

Pittsburgh Zoo and PPG Aquarium
One Wild Place
Pittsburgh, PA 15206
(412) 665–3640
www.pittsburghzoo.com

Open daily except Thanksgiving, Christmas, and New Year's Day

In June 2000 Pittsburgh added to its world-famous zoo a substantial public aquarium, the only one in Pennsylvania. The 45,000-square-foot facility includes forty aquatic exhibits awash in 380,000 gallons of salt and fresh water. More than 4,000 aquatic animals live here, and in keeping with the aquarium's emphasis on "Diversity of Water," they are drawn from habitats around the world. A river flows along the front of the new building, with waterfalls descending into a pool of North American fish. Inside, sharks and rays swim through simulated coral beds in a two-story 100,000-gallon tank. Elsewhere a rain forest exhibit allows visitors to experience a flooded Amazon, complete with piranhas and lush tropical foliage. A set of unique revolving tanks display jellyfish, electric eels, octopuses, and seahorses.

South Carolina

Ripley's Aquarium
1110 Celebrity Circle
Myrtle Beach, SC 29577
(800) 734-8888
www.ripleysaquarium.com

Open daily year-round

This $40 million coastal marine life display facility has much in common with Ripley's Aquarium of the Smokies in Gatlinburg, Tennessee. Intended primarily as a tourist attraction, it also offers educational opportunities. Of greatest appeal here are exhibits that place visitors in proximity to big sharks and other impressive sea animals. The Dangerous Reef exhibit includes a 750,000-gallon tank and a spectacular see-through tunnel. Other exhibits take visitors to tropical coral reefs, rain forests, and coastal tidelands. The aquarium presents dive shows and marine education classes hourly.

South Carolina Aquarium on Charleston Harbor
100 Aquarium Wharf
Charleston, SC 29401
(843) 720-1990
www.scaquarium.org

Open year-round except Thanksgiving, Christmas Eve, and Christmas Day

The South Carolina Aquarium takes visitors on a trip from the Blue Ridge Mountains to the waters of the Gulf Stream. Along the way they see and learn about thousands of creatures, including sharks, river otters, and a host of strange and unusual fish. Four distinct galleries of exhibits focus on the aquatic wildlife of the state's mountains, Piedmont region, coastal plain, and outer coast. Moving considerably farther afield, a relatively new exhibit presents the wonders of the Amazon. The aquarium sponsors conservation programs for local species, including sea turtles, bottle-nose dolphins, oysters, and ospreys, as well as extensive education and research programs.

Tennessee

Ripley's Aquarium of the Smokies
88 River Road
Gatlinburg, TN 37738
(865) 430-8808
www.ripleysaquariumofthesmokies.com

Open daily year-round

FOR OBVIOUS REASONS THESE CARDINALFISH AT THE DALLAS WORLD AQUARIUM OFTEN SEEK SHELTER IN OR NEAR SEA URCHINS.

Intended largely as tourist attractions, Ripley's Aquariums do an excellent job of bringing their visitors close to the animals. Exhibits emphasize the sensational and, for children especially, are a lot of fun. Menacing sharks surround visitors as they walk underwater through Dangerous Reef, a 750,000-gallon tank, on the world's longest moving glide path. At Ray Bay they can see rays and sharks from several viewing levels. Rainbow Rock features a stunning view of fish from Hawaii, Australia, and the Indian Ocean through a window the size of two movie screens. The rain forest exhibit features the deadly piranha of the Amazon region, while the Living Gallery shows off seahorses. At the Sea-For-Yourself Discovery Center, kids can experience the thrill of holding horseshoe crabs and similar interesting but harmless creatures. The aquarium presents dive shows and marine education classes hourly.

Tennessee Aquarium
1 Broad Street
P.O. Box 11048
Chattanooga, TN 37401
(423) 265-0695
www.tennesseeaquarium.com

Open daily except Thanksgiving and Christmas

The Tennessee Aquarium is unique in that an exceptionally large portion of the facility is given over to the celebration of freshwater species. Originally devoted entirely to freshwater habitats, the aquarium recently opened a new $30 million addition called Ocean Journey, which allows visitors to sample a variety of saltwater environments. Foremost among its exhibits may be the Secret Reef, a 618,000-gallon tank providing stunning views and insight into a coral reef ecosystem. Naturally there are plenty of predators in the tank, including tiger and sandbar sharks.

The original aquarium, now called the River Journey, specializes in fish, amphibians, and reptiles from the southeastern United States. Here visitors can see native trout and bass, water birds, and very large examples of the South's own inland sharklike predator—the alligator. The aquarium is actively involved in the conservation of many of the native species it displays, including alligators, turtles, crocodiles, and snakes.

Texas

Dallas World Aquarium
1801 North Griffon Street
Dallas, TX 75202
(214) 720-2224
www.dwazoo.com

Open daily except Thanksgiving and Christmas

As may be appropriate for a Texas aquarium, this one takes a big-state view of the world's oceans by trying with some success to span the globe. However, it does this with a relatively small amount of seawater, only about 85,000 gallons. That's a drop in the bucket compared with facilities such as the Shedd Aquarium in Chicago, where a single large tank contains more than thirty times that volume. Even so, the Dallas World Aquarium manages to delight visitors with a coral reef exhibit enlivened by a walk-through tunnel and an impressive assortment of smaller tanks detailing life from Palau, southern Australia and Lord

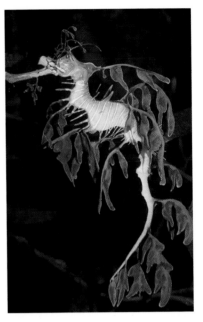

ALTHOUGH NAMED AFTER THE MONSTERS OF CHINESE MYTH, LEAFY SEA DRAGONS ARE NOT FEROCIOUS. THIS ONE LIVES AT THE DALLAS WORLD AQUARIUM.

Howe Island off New South Wales, the Solomon Islands, Fiji, the Bahamas, British Columbia, Sri Lanka, Indonesia, and Japan. The exhibits devoted to each of these regions manage on just 2,000 gallons each.

Among the aquarium highlights are a giant Pacific octopus with 8-foot-long tentacles, leafy sea dragons, moon jellies from Palau, the handsome paisley-patterned Mandarin dragonet from Indonesia, and a huge Japanese spider crab with a claw span of 13 feet. The Dallas World Aquarium is active in marine mammal, sea turtle, and seahorse conservation.

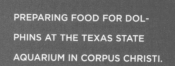
PREPARING FOOD FOR DOLPHINS AT THE TEXAS STATE AQUARIUM IN CORPUS CHRISTI.

Downtown Aquarium (Houston Aquarium)

410 Bagby Street
Houston, TX 77002
(713) 315-5000
www.downtownaquarium.com

Open days and evenings year-round

The Downtown Aquarium, better known to many as the Houston Aquarium, offers exhibits, rides, and special events with an underwater theme. The 500,000-gallon facility is the result of a redevelopment project combining two old Houston landmarks—Fire Station No. 1 and, appropriately enough, the Central Waterworks Building. A combination entertainment and educational facility, the six-acre complex includes two full-service restaurants, an assortment of child-friendly amusements, and exhibits displaying more than 200 species of marine life. Among the latter are stingrays, sea turtles, and a fish that literally walks on water. Exhibit galleries feature a number of habitats or background themes, including Caribbean reefs, the open Gulf of Mexico, the Amazon rain forest, an offshore oil rig, and a sunken Mayan temple.

San Antonio Zoo and Aquarium

3903 North Saint Mary's Street
San Antonio, TX 98212
(210) 734-7184
www.sazoo-aq.org

Open daily year-round

Part of a complex that includes the San Antonio Zoo, this aquarium contains a collection of more than 3,500 aquatic animals representing habitats around the world. A leader in promoting environmental conservation and education, the aquarium encourages public participation through its

THE TEXAS STATE AQUARIUM IS A MORE POPULAR TOURIST ATTRACTION THAN THE NEARBY USS *LEXINGTON*.

exhibits. For instance, a flooded Amazonian rain forest exhibit highlights the need to protect biodiversity. An exhibit on the Edward's Aquifer—the vast underground lake lying beneath several western states—raises local water conservation issues.

Natural settings showcase cranes and conservation efforts intended to protect these endangered water birds. The Pad, an amphibian exhibit, features rare and endangered frogs, toads, and salamanders along with interactive computers, videos, and lab equipment in a special "Amphi-Theater." The aquarium is active as a propagation facility for coral and the Lake Victoria cichlid. It also takes part in the Whooping Crane Recovery Program, flamingo rehabilitation in Mexico, and the protection of Kemp's Ridley sea turtles.

SeaWorld San Antonio

10500 SeaWorld Drive
San Antonio, TX 78251
(800) 700-7786
www.4adventure.com/seaworld/tx

Days and hours of operation vary by season

SeaWorld San Antonio presents an ocean-oriented entertainment package that combines amusement-park rides, a water park, special events, theater, and animal adventures. It's a little hard to imagine sea lions, belugas, rays, or sharks in Alamo country, but they can all be seen here. SeaWorld San Antonio has much in common with SeaWorlds located in Orlando and several additional destination cities around the country.

Texas State Aquarium
2710 North Shoreline Boulevard
Corpus Christi, TX 78402
(800) 477-GULF (4853)
www.texasstateaquarium.org

Open daily except Christmas and Thanksgiving

Overlooking the Gulf of Mexico, the Texas State Aquarium has a setting befitting a facility firmly focused on life in the Gulf. Entertainment, education, and conservation are all emphasized here, and the Gulf provides a wealth of material for aquarium programs, many of which encourage public participation. For instance, an active rehabilitation program for pelicans, sea turtles, and dolphins invites volunteers to care for sick or injured animals.

On the entertainment side, the aquarium dolphins are never a letdown, and teenagers may apply to participate in feedings by working

AN ESPECIALLY GREGARIOUS DOLPHIN GREETS TWO BOYS AT THE TEXAS STATE AQUARIUM.

with professional trainers at the aquarium's 400,000-gallon Dolphin Bay exhibit. Elsewhere visitors are introduced to the inhabitants of Texas's extensive salt marshes, tide pools, barrier islands, and coral reefs. Among the highlights are spiny porcupine fish, eels, and stingrays. There are also brightly colored coral reef fishes, river otters, seahorses, and jellyfish.

Virginia

Virginia Aquarium and Marine Science Center
717 General Booth Boulevard
Virginia Beach, VA 23451
(757) 437-4949
www.vmsm.com

Open daily year-round

The Virginia Aquarium and Marine Science Center celebrates Virginia's oceans, marshes, and the animals that live there with two separate pavilions loaded with fascinating exhibits. The Owls Creek Marsh Pavilion tells the story of life in a single salt marsh waterway—one that's located right beside the museum. Apparently there is a lot more life in Owls Creek than one might think; this pavilion's exhibits display river otters, fiddler crabs, seahorses, egrets, pelicans, royal terns, turkey vultures, great blue herons, and many other creatures. The birds are housed in an outdoor aviary. A nature trail links the Marsh Pavilion with the nearby Atlantic Ocean Pavilion, and the trail itself is one of the aquarium's best exhibits. Winding through more than ten acres of salt marsh, it provides a firsthand view of marine animals and water birds in their native environment.

THESE VISITORS MAY RIGHTLY FEEL THEY ARE HOLDING THE OCEAN IN THEIR HANDS WHEN VISITING THE TEXAS STATE AQUARIUM.

The Ocean Pavilion houses the aquarium's largest tanks, including the 300,000-gallon Norfolk Canyon exhibit, filled with tiger sharks, stingrays, and many large open-ocean fish, and the 70,000-gallon sea turtle tank. There are also separate jellyfish and octopus exhibits, a turtle hatching laboratory, and—a special feature of this aquarium—more than 300 hands-on displays.

Washington

Point Defiance Zoo and Aquarium
5400 North Pearl Street
Tacoma, WA 98407
(253) 591-5337
www.pdza.org

Open daily except Christmas

The dual aquariums at the Point Defiance Zoo and Aquarium offer visitors a chance to encounter the fascinating and beautiful aquatic creatures of the Northwest and Puget Sound, as well as the bright marine denizens of the South Pacific. Washington residents feel right at home in the Northwest Aquarium, which features such native species as salmon, rockfish, bay pipefish, and giant Pacific octopus. Its Around the Sound galleries bring to life both local landmarks and familiar marine habitats, such as native tide pool rocks festooned with urchins and anemones. A walk through the South Pacific Aquarium, on the other hand, reminds some visitors of their own tropical vacations. For divers especially it brings back memories of underwater adventures as it transports them through kingdoms of kelp, coral reef, and eelgrass.

The seahorse exhibits in the Pacific Aquarium are a special treat, and Point Defiance participates in international conservation programs aimed at protecting these strange but delicate creatures and their fragile environments. Whereas seahorses are made distinct by shape, many other sea creatures set themselves apart with color, a point that cannot be missed in the Pacific Aquarium's 24,000-gallon Lagoon exhibit. It is alive with some of nature's most brightly—some might say gaudily—painted fish. The Blue Hole exhibit is home to creatures that might prefer not to be seen at all, as much of the time they hide out in holes and crevasses. Perhaps the most popular exhibit is the Outer Reef environment, where as many as twenty sharks are constantly on patrol. Among these are lemon, nurse, tiger, whitetip reef, blacktip reef, woebegone, and sandbar sharks.

Visitors who want to know more about conservation, and an increasing number of them do, are pointed toward the Marine Discovery Center. There they can take part in educational programs focused on conservation, or perhaps pitch in with a donation.

Seattle Aquarium
1483 Alaskan Way
Pier 59
Seattle, WA 98101
(206) 386-4300
www.seattleaquarium.org

Open daily year-round

The mission statement of the Seattle Aquarium is a simple one: *Inspiring conservation of our marine environment*. The aquarium attempts to reach the widest possible audience for its conservation message, and its exhibits, displays, and educational initiatives are intended to engage

A LEAFY SEA DRAGON IS LIKELY HAPPY TO BE LOST AMONG THE KELP AND SEAWEED IN THIS POINT DEFIANCE EXHIBIT.

PUGET SOUND IS HOME TO THE LARGEST OCTOPUS SPECIES IN THE WORLD, AND VISITORS CAN SEE ONE UP CLOSE AT POINT DEFIANCE.

visitors of any age. Its many programs for preschoolers, adults, and seniors are meant to excite, involve, inform, and inspire a commitment to ocean conservation. Science camps, teacher trips, creative crafts, family adventures, beach naturalist walks, sea otter rescue programs, and a changing calendar of events and exhibits help bring the aquarium to the community and vice versa.

The aquarium complex is sizable and well designed. Some exhibits change from time to time, but the permanent ones are excellent. Among them are Life of a Drifter, featuring octopuses, jellies, and wolf eels; Myth, Magic, and Mystery, filled with fanciful creatures such as seahorses and sea dragons; and Life on the Edge, home to shorebirds and a thriving and colorful tide pool community. There are also tanks for crowd-pleasing seals and sea otters. One popular aquarium creature not on live display here is the orca, but visitors can get a close look at these "killer whales" by way of an innovative electronic display. Of particular interest to local visitors is the Puget Sound Fishes exhibit, which features such animals as grunt sculpins, Pacific spiny lumpsuckers, midshipmen fish, canary rockfish, wolf eels, and decorated warbonnets that live in waters within sight of downtown Seattle.

The aquarium's conservation efforts focus on both local and exotic species. The Aquarium Research Center currently conducts investigations into conservation and rehabilitation of sea otters, river otters, seabirds, giant octopuses, leafy sea dragons, sea turtles, and giant squids.

Photo Credits

Aquarium of the Pacific, Long Beach, California: pp. 119 (top, bottom right), 120 (top right, left); © Marj Awai: p. 105; © David Bull/Audubon Nature Institute: p. 132 (bottom); Birch Aquarium at Scripps Institution of Oceanography: pp. 100, 120 (bottom right), 121, 122 (left); © Bruce Carlson: pp. 84 (insert), 103 (bottom), 104 (top), 112 (top), 113 (top), 115; © Jennifer Crites: p. 98 (top); The Dallas World Aquarium: pp. 140–41; © J. C. Delbeek: pp. i (right), x (top), 85 (left, right), 87, 89–90, 91 (bottom), 96, 108 (top), 109 (top, bottom left), 113 (bottom), 123 (top), 129 (top); © D. DeMello/WCS: p. 136 (left); © G. Fisher/NYA: p. 136 (top right); © G. R. Horn: p. 135 (moray); © Darren Jew/Living Image: pp. 128 (center right, bottom), 129 (bottom); © Grahm Jones, Columbus Zoo and Aquarium: pp. 23, 138–39; © Alice Keesing: pp. 106, 110–11, 114, 116; © J. Maher/WCS: p. 135 (sea lion, seal); The Maritime Aquarium at Norwalk: pp. 124, 125 (center left), 127 (top right); Monterey Bay Aquarium: pp. 54 (inset), 55 (right), 58, 60, 61 (left), 62, 66, 69, 72 (bottom), 74 (bottom), 75 (second from top, bottom), 122 (top right, bottom right), 123 (center right); Monterey Bay Aquarium/R. R. Jones: p. 67 (top right); Monterey Bay Aquarium/Rob Lewine: p. 68 (second from top); Monterey Bay Aquarium/Doc White: p. 74 (top); Monterey Bay Aquarium/Randy Wilder: pp. 54 (background), 55 (moray, shark, jellyfish), 57, 63–65, 67 (bottom left), 73, 76–77, 78 (top), 80–81, 82 (top), 83, 123 (bottom left); Courtesy Mote Marine Aquarium: pp. 126 (left), 127 (bottom); Courtesy Mystic Aquarium and Institute for Exploration: pp. 125 (top right, center right, bottom left, bottom right), 126 (top right); National Aquarium in Baltimore: pp. 35, 133 (bottom); New England Aquarium: pp. 17, 28, 29 (three photos on left), 30–34, 36 (two bottom), 38 (left top and bottom), 39, 40 (middle two), 41, 42 (left), 43 (top), 44 (second from top, bottom), 45 (bottom), 46 (left), 48–53, 134, 148 (second from right); Newport Aquarium, Kentucky: pp. 131 (top, bottom); North Carolina Aquarium at Fort Fisher: pp. 136 (bottom), 137; Courtesy Point Defiance Zoo and Aquarium, Tacoma: pp. 144–45; © John E. Randall: pp. i (second from left), v (right), 85 (second from left), 97 (left), 109 (right), 117 (right), 128 (top), 148 (second from left); © Todd Stailey, Tennessee Aquarium: p. 79 (right); © Shedd Aquarium/www.fishphotos.org: pp. i (starfish, dolphin), iii, iv, v (three on left), vi, viii, ix, x (two bottom), xi, xii, 1–2, 4, 5 (bottom three), 6 (bottom), 7–8, 9 (bottom three), 10, 11 (top), 12–13, 14 (top), 15 (top and bottom), 16 (top), 18, 19 (bottom left), 20 (top), 21–22, 24–27, 130, 131 (center), 132 (top right), 133 (top right), 146, 147, 148 (left); Texas State Aquarium: pp. 142–43; © Tim Walsh, Tennessee Aquarium: p. 79 (left); © Jacob Wettstein, Alaska SeaLife Center, Seward: pp. 118, 119 (bottom left, bottom center); Waikiki Aquarium: pp. vii, 84 (background), 85 (second from right), 86, 88 (bottom), 92–93, 97 (right), 99 (top), 102 (top), 103 (top), 107 (top left, bottom left), 112 (bottom)

Video captures courtesy Driftwood Productions

About the Authors

  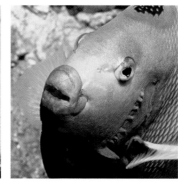 

John Grant is the producer or executive producer of more than forty hours of documentary programs seen on public television, including *Legendary Lighthouses, West Point: The First 200 Years, Great Lodges of the National Parks, The Homes of FDR,* and *America's Scenic Rail Journeys.* He is producer-director of the *Window to the Sea* documentary for the Public Broadcasting Service (PBS). Grant is the author or coauthor of six companion books to his television programs, including the award-winning *Great American Rail Journeys.*

Ray Jones is the author or coauthor of nearly thirty books on natural history, American culture, and lighthouses, including the award-winning *Lighthouse Encyclopedia* and *Legendary Lighthouses,* the best-selling companion to the PBS series. A former writing coach for *Southern Living* magazine and senior editor for Time-Life Books, he lives in Pebble Beach, California, where he continues to write and serves as a publishing consultant.

This book is the authors' third collaboration.